Super Easy Recipes
For Everyone

111 Quick And Simple Dishes You Will Love

Slavka Bodic

Copyright @2020

All rights reserved. No part of this book may be reproduced in any form without writing permission in writing from the author. Reviewers may quote brief passages in reviews.

No part of this publication may be reproduced or transmitted in any form or by any means, mechanical or electronic, including photocopying or recording, or by any information storage and retrieval system, or transmitted by email without permission in writing from the publisher. While all attempts have been made to verify the information provided in this publication, neither the author nor the publisher assumes any responsibility for errors, omissions or contrary interpretations of the subject matter herein.

This book is for entertainment purposes only. The views expressed are those of the author alone and should not be taken as expert instruction or command. The reader is responsible for his or her actions. Adherence to all applicable laws and regulations, including international, federal, state and local governing professional licensing, business practices, advertising, and all other aspects of doing business in US, Canada or any other jurisdiction is the sole responsibility of the purchaser or reader.

Neither the author nor the publisher assumes any responsibility or liability whatsoever on the behalf of the purchaser or reader of these materials. Any perceived slight of any individual or organization is purely unintentional. Similarity with already published recipes is possible.

Imprint: Independently published

Please sign up for free Balkan and Mediterranean recipes:
www.balkanfood.org

Introduction

Even today, when most people are very much aware what so-called "convenient" food consists of, many still believe that cooking requires an exceptional level of skill, not to mention time and effort. Luckily, *that's not exactly true*! Even if they're complete beginners, any person out there can master these 111 recipes — and yes, that means you too!

One of the major complaints we often hear about cooking is that it takes too much time and that the results are never as good as the stuff we can order from restaurants, fast food joints, etc. But for anything to be good in this world, we do have to put our time and effort into it.

Does that mean that cooking is difficult and reserved for the most talented among us? Of course not! Cooking as an activity can be both a hobby and a career, but it doesn't always have to entail some extraordinary talent and skills worthy of Michelin-rated restaurants.

This book isn't going to make you into a bona fide chef à la Gordon Ramsay and the like. It will, however, change the way you live your life, your diet, health, and more.

These beginner-friendly recipes are for those who have long been afraid of not only experimenting but also cooking simple dishes at home. It's the ultimate resource for fast-food lovers and people who have Chinese takeout on speed dial. Moreover, it's the be-all and end-all for aspiring home cooks, working professionals, busy parents and grandparents, independent teenagers, and anyone else who wishes to discover the magic of cooking!

Of course, you probably won't stop ordering takeout every once in a while, just because you know how to cook. However, cooking by yourself and actually knowing which ingredients go with what, as well as how to whip up a quick lunch or dinner, ought to be more rewarding (at least!).

Through these recipes, your fear of your kitchen will slowly dissipate. You will gain the confidence necessary to feed yourself and your loved ones with homecooked, healthy food that usually doesn't take more than 40 minutes to make. Better yet, you will get to enjoy recipes that are so easy to make that you won't even feel like you're doing something out of necessity. In fact, in time, you'll start enjoying cooking and embrace the calmness and focus it gives you!

As they say, practice makes perfect; soon enough, you will master these super-easy recipes for beginners and be ready to move onto more complicated concoctions. But even when that happens, this book will remain a true friend to you.

Once your confidence grows and you have tried most, if not, all of the simple yet delicious recipes found here, you'll be able to introduce your very own variations. By just changing or adding several ingredients, you will elevate your cooking and truly master flavors, textures, and scents. Thus, each dish will be a mouth-watering experience you can be proud of. After all, it will be a product of your excellent skills, time, and effort!

Cooking for yourself and your loved ones doesn't have to be a chore. It shouldn't make you nervous right off the bat. Nobody was born with exceptional cooking skills; we all had to hone them over time, even the best chefs!

If you want to know how to cook dishes that are not only easy to make but embody the basics of cooking, you've found the right book. In the following pages, you will see that cooking is not as difficult as some make it out to be. It's definitely something *anyone* can master with enough time and effort, no matter how clumsy or unimaginative they think they are. Besides, the more you cook something, the better you become at it!

Beginners or not, super-easy recipes are at your fingertips and will change your perspective on food, ingredient combinations, and cooking. Over time, you will also recognize which ones are more your style and build upon them. Soon enough, you will be figuring out new flavors and implementing your very own ideas.

If you're ready, let's set off on this journey together. Here are 111 recipes for beginners to get you started in the kitchen today!

Table of Contents

INTRODUCTION 3

BREAKFAST 10

    FRENCH OMELET WITH CAVIAR 11

    EUROPEAN SCRAMBLED EGGS 12

    CHANTERELLE OMELET WITH THYME AND ROSEMARY 13

    CANAPÉ CROSTINI 15

    SYRIAN OMELET 16

APPETIZERS 17

    FRIED CHEESE 18

    ARMENIAN LAVASH CHEESE STICKS 19

    BATTERED CALAMARI 20

    FRENCH BREAD APPETIZER 21

    SMOKED SALMON ROSES 22

    TOMATOES WITH PROSCIUTTO 23

    APPETIZER WITH SPINACH 24

    HAM AND CHEESE LAVASH POCKETS 25

    FRIED EGGPLANTS WITH POMEGRANATE SEEDS 26

    EGGS WITH SPINACH 27

DIPS 28

    GREEK SKORDALIA 29

    LAYERED EGGPLANT DIP 30

    TURKISH CACIK 31

    MUHAMMARA 32

    BEET DIP 33

    MUSHROOM CAVIAR 34

    ZUCCHINI DIP 35

    LEMON GARLIC DIP 36

SOUPS 37

    Lentil And Noodle Soup 38

    Potato Soup... 39

    Spinach Cream Soup 40

    Tourain Du Perigord.. 41

    Italian Buttery Onion Soup 42

    Turkish Highland Meadow Soup 43

    Vegetable Soup 44

    Greek Lentil Soup 45

MAIN DISHES 46

    Creole Rice Pilaf 47

    Yogurt Pasta 48

    Romanian Goulash... 49

    Cabbage With Noodles 50

    Sweet Chicken With Cherry Sauce 51

    Russian Chicken Shashlik In Nut Marinade 53

    Steamed Salmon With Parsley Sauce 54

    Spicy Potato Quesadillas 55

    Fast And Easy Pork Sausage 56

    Italian Grilled Shrimp Skewers... 57

    Meatballs In Garlic Yogurt Sauce 58

    Shrimp And Vegetable Clay Pot Casserole 60

    Cauliflower Stew.. 61

    Chicken Potato Stew.. 62

    Russian Piroshki.. 63

    Mushroom Julienne 64

    Trout With Honey, Mustard And Lemon 65

    Tofu Crunchies.. 66

    Bulgur Wheat Pilaf 67

    Vegan Margherita Pizza 68

    Hummus Pasta With Orange 69

    Pasta Tomatina... 70

Spicy Potato Curry 71

Chicken Thighs With Lemon 72

Chicken Piccata 73

Quick Stew 74

Syrian Mejaddarah 75

Sautéed Broad Beans 76

Rice With Pomegranate.. 77

Chicken Breast Ragout With Mushrooms.................................. 78

Fish Pie 79

Russian Beef With Veggies 80

Shrimp Pan With Parsley, Lemon, And Garlic........................ 81

Cashew Zoodles 82

Spanish Chicken Pan 83

French Pilaf With Mushrooms.. 84

Caucasus Beef Kebab 85

Spanish Pepper Noodle Pan.. 86

Salmon With Tarragon Leaves 87

Baba Ganouj 88

Zucchini Tomato Stew 89

Spanish Potatoes 90

Gambas In Garlic Oil.. 91

Manchego Balls With Paprika Salsa 92

Armenian Johob 93

Chicken Apricots Stir Fry.. 94

Beetroot Pasta 95

Lime And Herby Baked Fish 96

Persian Herbed Frittatas.. 97

Chicken With Saffron.. 98

Stew With Potato And Rice.. 99

SALADS..100

Zucchini Orzo Salad..101

Twirls Salad..102

GREEK HOT POTATO SALAD 103

MUSHROOM SALAD 104

CARROTS SAUTÉ 105

POMEGRANATE ORANGE AND BABY SPINACH SALAD 106

CARROT AND ORANGE SALAD 107

FRENCH-STYLE POTATO SALAD 108

DESSERTS **109**

GREEK BUTTER BISCUITS 110

ITALIAN COOKIES 111

CHOCOLATE BALLS 112

GREEK RICE PUDDING 113

AMARETTI COOKIES 114

SUGAR COOKIES 115

SYRIAN HARISSA 116

SYRIAN MILK PUDDING 117

CARAMELIZED DATES 118

SUNSET FRUIT SALAD 119

CHOCOLATE MOUSSE 120

TURKISH BAKED RICE PUDDING 121

KAZANDIBI 123

CREAMY COCOA 124

NIRVANA CHOCOLATE PUDDING 125

STRAWBERRY AND ORANGE SKEWERS 126

TURKISH SWEET CHURROS 127

MINT AND WATERMELON ICE CREAM 129

TURKISH CATAL 130

PERSIAN RICE COOKIES 131

WALNUT CAKE 133

ONE LAST THING **138**

Breakfast

French Omelet With Caviar

Preparation time: 15 minutes
Cook time: 10 minutes
Nutrition facts (per serving): 169 kcal (5.3g fat, 14g protein, 0g fiber)

Ingredients (2 servings)

3 tablespoons pressed caviar
2 tablespoons sour cream
1 tablespoon minced chives
2 large eggs
1 tablespoon unsalted butter
Salt and black pepper, to taste

Preparation

Spread the caviar between two sheets of plastic into a 1/8-inch-thick (5 x 8-inch) rectangle. Cut half of this rectangle into 1/2-inch strips. Chop the remaining caviar and transfer to a small mixing bowl. Add in the sour cream and chives. Beat all the eggs in a small mixing bowl until frothy and add salt and black pepper for seasoning. Melt butter in 6-inch nonstick skillet over high heat. Pour the eggs and constantly stir with a rubber spatula, until the eggs are set. Remove from heat, add a dollop of the sour cream mixture at the center of the eggs. Shake the skillet again to loosen the omelet, and then fold 1/3 of the egg over the cream filling. Flip the cream omelet onto a plate, folding it over itself. Garnish with the caviar and serve.

European Scrambled Eggs

Preparation time: 15 minutes
Cook time: 10 minutes
Nutrition facts (per serving): 256 kcal (6g fat, 9g protein, 6g fiber)

Ingredients (12 servings)
12 large eggs
1/4 cup 2 tablespoons water
6 tablespoons cold butter, diced
2 teaspoons white truffle oil
1 tablespoon chives, finely chopped
6 warmed brioche rolls, toasted
Sea salt and black pepper, to taste

Preparation
Mix and beat the eggs with water in a suitable bowl. Melt 2 tablespoons butter in a stainless-steel bowl set over a pot of boiling water. Stir in the eggs and cook on low heat while stirring with a rubber spatula for about 5 minutes. Add the remaining butter to the eggs and cook for about 5 minutes. Season with salt and black pepper and then transfer to plates. Garnish with truffle oil, chives, and serve warm with brioche.

Chanterelle Omelet With Thyme and Rosemary

Preparation time: 15 minutes
Cooking time: 10 minutes
Nutritional Facts (per serving): 267 kcal (21 g protein, 14 g fiber, 18 g fat)

Ingredients (2 servings)

7 ounces fresh chanterelles
2 green onions
2 cloves garlic
3-4 spring thyme
2 sprigs rosemary
1 tablespoon olive oil
1 tablespoon butter
4 eggs
4 tablespoons milk
Salt and pepper
Some parsley or chives

Preparation

Clean the chanterelles. Cut the green onions into rings, grate the garlic cloves, remove the thyme and rosemary leaves from the stems and chop finely. Heat the oil in a non-stick pan. Add the mushrooms, green onions, garlic, and herbs to the pan and cook over high heat for a few minutes. Adjust the flavor with salt and pepper. Remove from pan and keep warm while you cook the eggs.

Wipe the pan clean with kitchen paper. Melt the butter in the pan. Beat the eggs with the milk and some salt and pepper. Pour the egg mixture into the pan, reduce the heat, and cook the omelet until it starts to set. It depends on how dry you want it; it could be a bit runny in the middle of it could be firmer and drier if you prefer. My son and I prefer it a bit less dry, but my daughter likes it dry, so it's a matter of taste.

When the Omelet is almost set but not completely dry, spread the chanterelle mixture over one half of the Omelet. Fold the other half over the mushrooms with a wide spatula. Turn off the heat and let it rest in the pan for another minute or two. Cut in half, sprinkle with parsley or chives and serve with bread and green salad.

Canapé Crostini

Preparation time: 5 minutes
Cook time: 8 minutes
Nutrition facts (per serving): 231 kcal (10g fat, 2g protein, 6g fiber)

Ingredients (4 servings)

Crostini base
1 baguette
Extra virgin olive oil
1 garlic clove

Topping
2 large ripe tomatoes
Extra virgin olive oil
Small handful basil leaves
Salt and black pepper, to taste
honey, for drizzling

Preparation

At 375 degrees F, preheat your oven. Cut the baguette into 1-inch thick diagonal slices. Place these slices on a baking sheet, drizzle oil on top, and bake for 8 minutes. For the tomato, basil, and mint topping, chop the tomatoes and add them to a small bowl. Drizzle the oil, basil, and mint leaves, salt, black pepper, and sugar. Toss everything together. To assemble, simply spread the tomato mixture on top of eight crostini. Garnish with honey. Serve.

Syrian Omelet

Preparation time: 10 minutes
Cook time: 5 minutes
Nutrition facts (per serving): 268 kcal (2g fat, 19g protein, 0.3g fiber)

Ingredients (6 servings)
6 large eggs
15 tablespoons flour
1 bunch parsley, chopped
1 large chopped onion
1/2 cup olive oil
1/4 teaspoon ground red pepper
1/2 tablespoon salt
Black pepper to taste

Preparation
Beat the eggs with onion and parsley in a bowl. Add spices, salt, and flour then mix well until smooth and thick. Heat 3 tablespoons olive oil in a cooking skillet and add 1/3 cup of batter into the skillet. Cook for 2 minutes per side. Continue making more *Ojji* with the remaining batter. Serve warm.

Appetizers

Fried Cheese

Preparation time: 10 minutes
Cook time: 20 minutes

Ingredients (7 servings)

1/2 pound kasseri or similar cheese (sliced 1/2 inch thick)
2 tablespoons brandy
4 tablespoons butter
1 well beaten egg
1 teaspoon flour
Juice of 1/2 lemon

Preparation

Heat the butter in a large heavy skillet over moderate heat. Beat the egg and flour together and dip the cheese slices into the mixture. Fry until well browned on both sides. Remove from the heat and add the brandy.

Carefully ignite the brandy with a match and shake the skillet until the flame is extinguished. Squeeze the lemon juice over the cheese and serve directly from the skillet with crusty bread.

Armenian Lavash Cheese Sticks

Preparation time: 10 minutes
Cook time: 5 minutes
Nutrition facts: 1 serving 354 kcal (18g protein, 7g fat, 46g carbs)

Ingredients (2 servings)

2 eggs
2 strips of any cheese
2 tablespoon butter
1 teaspoon chopped garlic
1 teaspoon chopped dill
1 piece Armenian lavash or similar cheese

Preparation

Cut the cream cheese into thin strips and beat the eggs well. Chop the garlic and chop the dill finely. Cut the lavash into strips. Then we take a strip of the lavash, put two strips of cheese on it along its length and a little garlic. Next, sprinkle with herbs on top and carefully roll the strip into a roll. Dip the resulting sticks in an egg and fry in butter on both sides until they reach a roasted golden color. It should take 4-6 minutes. Serve to the table with herbs and sour cream.

Battered Calamari

Preparation time: 10 minutes
Cooking time: 5 minutes
Nutrition facts (per serving): 209 kcal (fats 8.6g, proteins 13.9g, fibers 0.8g)

Ingredients (6 servings)
1 cup of buttermilk
2 cups of vegetable oil
1 pound of squid, cut into rings
½ tablespoon of ground black pepper
1 cup of flour
½ tablespoon of salt
1 teaspoon of dried oregano

Preparation
Combine the flour, pepper, salt and oregano in a bowl. Add the buttermilk into another bowl and dip in the squid rings, then dip them into the flour mixture. Deep-fry the coated pieces in hot oil in batches until they are evenly browned. Place them on a paper towel to drain and serve.

French Bread Appetizer

Preparation time: 10 minutes
Cook time: 10 minutes
Nutrition facts (per serving): 130 kcal (8g fat, 2g protein, 1.1g fiber)

Ingredients (4 servings)
1 baguette
24 ounces goat cheese
3 tart apples
4 tablespoons heavy cream
Black pepper, to taste
Mixture of dried herbs (Herbes de Provence), to taste

Preparation
Slice the baguette in half, lengthwise. Spread the cream on both halves of the bread. Peel, core, and slice all the apples. Spread the apple slices on the bread. Add the goat cheese over the apple slices. Sprinkle pepper and dried herbs on top. Bake in for about 10 minutes at 350 degrees F. Cut each half into about 12 pieces. Serve.

Smoked Salmon Roses

Preparation time: 10 minutes
Nutrition facts (per serving): 71 kcal (3g fat, 14g protein, 4g fiber)

Ingredients (2 servings)
5 ounces rye bread, toasted
3 1/2 ounces half-fat crème Fraiche
3 1/2 ounces light cream cheese
1 lemon, zest, and juice
2 tablespoon fresh chives, chopped
1 tablespoon fresh dill,
3 1/2 ounces smoked salmon

Preparation
Using a round cookie cutter, cut rounds from the rye bread. Beat the cream cheese, crème Fraiche, and lemon juice using an electric hand mixer until smooth. Fold in fresh herbs and salt. Transfer the cream filling into a piping bag with a star-shaped nozzle and pipe onto each rye bread round. Roll up a slice of salmon and curl out their edges to make a rose. Place one on top of each canape and garnish with zest and dill. Serve.

Tomatoes With Prosciutto

Preparation time: 10 minutes
Cook time: 15 minutes
Nutrition facts (per serving): 172 kcal (7.9g protein, 11g fat, 31g carbs)

Ingredients (2 servings)

6 pieces prosciutto
3 cloves garlic
1 piece of chili pepper
1 teaspoon thyme
1 teaspoon rosemary
1 teaspoon balsamic cream
1 teaspoon sugar
1 teaspoon Olive oil
Salt to taste
Ground black pepper to taste
15 oz small tomatoes

Preparation

From 4 layers of foil, form a square container and put the tomatoes in it. Pour the olive oil, and then add sprigs of thyme and rosemary. Cut chili pepper, crush and peel the garlic, and then place them on the bottom of the bowl. Pour the tomatoes with balsamic cream. Sprinkle the tomatoes with sugar, salt, and pepper. Bake the tomatoes in preheated to 360 F in normal mode or with convection for 16 minutes. Cool the tomatoes, put them on a plate, pour the allocated juice, and serve with prosciutto.

Appetizer With Spinach

Preparation time: 15 minutes
Cook time: 5 minutes
Nutrition facts (per serving): 225 kcal (8g protein, 16g fat, 52g carbs)

Ingredients (4 servings)
17 oz spinach
7 oz onions
3 oz walnuts
1 green chili pepper
2 cloves of garlic
12 branches cilantro
3 pieces of parsley
Pomegranate kernels to taste
2 tablespoon wine vinegar
Salt to taste

Preparation
Boil the spinach for 5 minutes. Then place in a colander, put on paper towels, and allow it to cool. Finely chop onion, garlic, pepper, cilantro, and parsley. When the spinach has cooled, process it in the meat grinder together with the nuts. Stir everything until smooth, adding wine vinegar and salt. Give it a beautiful shape as balls, put on a plate, and garnish with pomegranate seeds and serve.

Ham And Cheese Lavash Pockets

Preparation time: 10 minutes
Cook time: 20 minutes
Nutrition facts (per serving): 214 kcal (12g protein, 22g fat, 19g carbs)

Ingredients (6 servings)

6 eggs
5.2 oz. cheese
7oz ham
Green onions to taste
1 piece of Armenian lavash
2 cups of water

Preparation

Boil eggs in 2 cups of water for 15 minutes. Grate the cheese on a coarse grater, finely chop the ham, add chopped onions and boiled eggs. Cut each sheet of lavash into 4-6 parts. Wrap the stuffing in them. Fry in a pan on both sides for 3 minutes and then serve.

Fried Eggplants With Pomegranate Seeds

Preparation time: 15 minutes
Cook time: 10 minutes
Nutrition facts (per serving): 121 kcal (1.2g protein, 8g fat, 19g carbs)

Ingredients (5 servings)
3 eggplant
1 bunch cilantro
3 cloves of garlic
½ grenade
¼ cup refined oil
Salt to taste

Preparation
Cut the stalk from the eggplant and, without removing the peel, cut into lengthwise slices ¼ inch thick. Heat the pan, pour oil on it, and fry the eggplants for about 5 minutes on each side.
Crush the garlic, cilantro and salt thoroughly in a mortar until you get a smooth consistency. Coat each fried eggplant slice on both sides with paste and put on a dish. Sprinkle the eggplant with pomegranate seeds before serving.

Eggs With Spinach

Preparation time: 10 minutes
Cook time: 10 minutes
Nutrition facts (per serving): 125 kcal (8g protein, 8.9g fat, 3g carbs)

Ingredients (4 servings)
1 pound of spinach
2 eggs
1 tablespoon butters
5 green onions stems
2 tablespoon parsley
2 tablespoon cilantro
Salt and pepper to taste

Preparation
Boil the spinach in a cup of water for 5 minutes, then dry it, and set aside. Finely dice all the greenery. Take a pan add butter, spinach, and the diced greenery. Stir for 30 seconds, then break the eggs on them, and stir. Cook for 3 minutes and serve.

Dips

Greek Skordalia

Preparation time: 10 minutes
Cook time: 15 minutes

Ingredients (2 servings)

8 oz. russet potatoes, peeled and cut into 2″ pieces
1/2 cups walnuts (and more for serving)
2 peeled cloves garlic
3 tablespoon lemon juice
2 tablespoon white wine vinegar
1/2 cups extra-virgin olive oil (and more for serving)
2 tablespoon freshly chopped parsley for serving
Pita bread and cucumber spears for serving
Salt

Preparation

In a large pot, cover the potatoes with water and season generously with salt. Bring to a boil and cook until totally soft, 12 to 14 minutes. Drain and let cool. Meanwhile, add the walnuts to a food processor. Grate the garlic over the walnuts and process, while drizzling in the lemon juice and vinegar, until the nuts are thoroughly ground.

Add the cooled potato and olive oil and process until a thick but creamy spread form, also adding a few splashes of water to thin, if needed. Season well with salt. Top with olive oil, chopped walnuts, and parsley. Serve with bread and cucumbers.

Layered Eggplant Dip

Preparation time: 15 minutes
Cook time: 20 minutes
Nutrition facts (per serving): 249 kcal (7g fat, 9g protein, 3g fiber)

Ingredients (8 servings)
2 cups *Mutabal*
1/2-pound ground beef
1 can (14 oz) diced tomato
1 tablespoon tomato paste
1 medium onion, chopped
2 tablespoons olive oil
Half a bunch parsley, cleaned and chopped
1/4 teaspoon *Bharat* (Syrian Spice Mix)
Salt and black pepper, to taste

Preparation
Sauté the onion with oil in a cooking pan until soft. Stir in the meat and cook until brown. Stir in the tomato paste, salt, black pepper, and diced tomato then cook for 15 minutes on a simmer. Add 1/2 *Mutabal* at the bottom of a casserole dish, add the beef mixture on top, and spread the remaining *Mutabal* on top of the beef. Serve.

Turkish Cacik

Preparation time: 10 minutes
Nutrition facts (per serving): 64 kcal

Ingredients (4 servings)
2 cups of cold plain yogurt
3 medium-sized grated cucumbers (wring out the excess water)
2 cloves of garlic, finely chopped
1 tablespoon of extra-virgin olive oil
1 cup of cold water
1/2 teaspoon of pepper
1 tablespoon of fresh mint, chopped
1/2 teaspoon of dried oregano

Preparation
Pour the olive oil and yogurt in a small mixing bowl and whisk until smooth. Add a little bit of cold water and whisk into a required thick paste. Add the grated cucumbers, chopped garlic, 1/2 teaspoon of pepper, dried oregano and chopped mint. Mix well and serve.

Muhammara

Preparation time: 10 minutes
Cook time: 30 minutes
Nutrition facts (per serving): 130 kcal (8g fat, 2g protein, 1.1g fiber)

Ingredients (8 servings)
2 red bell peppers
4 tablespoon olive oil
1/4-pound shelled toasted walnuts
1 garlic clove, chopped
2 1/2 tablespoon tomato paste
3/4 cup breadcrumbs
2 tablespoon pomegranate molasses
1 teaspoon Aleppo pepper
1/2 teaspoon sugar
1 teaspoon sumac
1/2 teaspoon salt
1/2 teaspoon cayenne pepper

Preparation
At 425 degrees F, preheat the oven. Rub the prepared bell peppers with 1 tablespoon olive oil and place it in a baking sheet. Roast these peppers for 30 minutes in the preheated oven. Flip the peppers once cooked halfway through. Transfer the roasted red peppers to a bowl and cover with a plastic wrap. Leave for 10 minutes, then peel the peppers. Remove all the pepper's seeds and cut the peppers into strips. Transfer the strips to a blender and add 3 tablespoon olive oil, tomato paste, walnuts, breadcrumbs, Aleppo pepper, sumac, sugar, cayenne, and salt. Finally, blend until smooth. Serve.

Beet Dip

Preparation time: 10 minutes
Cook time: 10 minutes
Nutrition facts (per serving): 71 kcal (3g fat, 2g protein, 4g fiber)

Ingredients (6 servings)
2 big beets
2 tablespoons tahini
1 glove mashed garlic
3 tablespoons lemon juice
2 tablespoons olive oil
Salt and black pepper to taste

Preparation
Boil the beet in a pot filled with water until soft, then drain, and transfer to a blender jug. Add tahini, lemon juice, garlic, olive oil, salt, and black pepper. Blend until smooth and then serve.

Mushroom Caviar

Preparation time: 10 minutes
Cooking time: 10 minutes
Nutrition facts (per serving): 295 kcal (fats 28g, proteins 3g, fibers 2g)

Ingredients (2 servings)
4 ¼ ounces (130 g) of dried mushrooms
1 onion, chopped
4 tablespoons of sunflower oil
2 garlic cloves, minced
2 tablespoons of 5% vinegar
Salt and black pepper to taste

Preparation
Soak the mushrooms in cold water for 3 hours, then drain. Reserve the cooking liquid. Rinse and finely chop all the mushrooms. Now, add the chopped mushrooms to the reserved cooking liquid. Cook the mushrooms until the liquid has completely evaporated. Sauté the onions in a pan, then add the mushrooms, garlic, vinegar, oil, black pepper and salt, sauté for another 10 minutes. Mix well and serve.

Zucchini Dip

Preparation time: 15 minutes
Cook time: 11 minutes
Nutrition facts (per serving): 146 kcal (11g fat, 9g protein, 0.1g fiber)

Ingredients (8 servings)

1-pound (500 g) zucchini squash
4 cloves garlic
1 chopped small onion
Juice of 1 lemon
5 tablespoons olive oil
1 tablespoon dried mint
Salt and black pepper, to taste

Preparation

Add the zucchini to a colander and drizzle salt on top. Leave them to drain all the liquid out of it. Sauté the onion and garlic with 3 tablespoon oil in a cooking pot for 1 minute. Stir in zucchini and the remaining ingredients. Mix well and cook for about 10 minutes with occasional stirring. Mix well and mash the zucchini mixture with a hand masher. Serve warm with olive oil on top.

Lemon Garlic Dip

Preparation time: 10 minutes
Nutrition facts (per serving): 60 kcal (7g fat, 0g protein, 0g fiber)

Ingredients (6 servings)
Juice of 1 lemon
4 cloves of smashed garlic
1 tablespoon olive oil
A pinch of ground black pepper
1/4 teaspoon salt

Preparation
Add and blend all the lemon dip's ingredients in a blender until smooth. Serve.

Soups

Lentil And Noodle Soup

Preparation time: 15 minutes
Cook time: 30 minutes
Nutrition facts (per serving): 278 kcal (11g fat, 13g protein, 1.2g fiber)

Ingredients (4 servings)
1 onion, chopped
1 carrot, chopped
1 cup red lentils
1 lemon, juiced
1 teaspoon curry powder
1 teaspoon ground coriander
1 teaspoon salt
3 tablespoon olive oil
3 cups boiling water
3 1/2 ounces (100g) fine noodles

Preparation
Sauté the onions, carrot, and olive oil in a large saucepan until soft. Add the lentils, spices, salt, noodles and water to the pot. Cook for 30 minutes on a low heat. Add lemon juice, mix well and serve warm.

Potato Soup

Preparation time: 10 minutes
Cooking Time: 20 minutes
Nutrition facts (per serving): 412 kcal

Ingredients (2 servings)
2 cups of medium-sized potato cubes
2 tablespoons of fresh lemon juice
1 small finely chopped onion
1 cup of carrot cubes
1 1/2 tablespoons of all-purpose flour
½ cup of cubanelle pepper, chopped into cubes
1/2 teaspoon of fresh lemon zest
2 tablespoons of melted butter
Salt to taste
1 bay leaf
2 1/2 cups of homemade chicken stock
1/2 teaspoon of pepper
2 tablespoons of chopped parsley

Preparation
Put the melted butter in a pan and fry the onion and carrot together for 4 minutes on medium heat. Now add potato cubes, stir for 4-5 minutes. Add all-purpose flour and stir for another minute, now add the chicken stock, cubanelle pepper, salt and pepper. Let it simmer on low heat until the carrots soften. Add the parsley, lemon juice and lemon zest in. Take out the bay leaf, garnish and serve hot.

Spinach Cream Soup

Preparation Time: 2 minutes
Cooking Time: 20 minutes
Nutrition facts (per serving): 310 kcal

Ingredients (4 servings)
1 1/3 pounds of spinach, washed, drained
1/4 teaspoon of paprika
1/2 teaspoon of salt
1 garlic clove, chopped
2 tablespoons of plain flour
1 tablespoon of butter
1 onion, chopped
2 tablespoons of plain flour
1/4 teaspoon of pepper
4 tablespoons of heavy cream
1 garlic clove, chopped
3 cups of chicken stock
1 tablespoon of lemon juice

Preparation
In a deep saucepan, sauté the onion with the butter for 3 minutes on a medium flame. Add the chopped garlic and sauté for about one more minute. Add the plain flour, stir and slowly pour the chicken stock in it while stirring constantly, so that there are no lumps. When it starts to boil add the spinach, lemon juice, paprika, salt and pepper. Cook over medium heat for 16-19 minutes. Pour it into the blender and blend until smooth. Put a tablespoon of cream on top and serve with bread slices.

Tourain Du Perigord

Preparation time: 10 minutes
Cook time: 15 minutes
Nutrition facts (per serving): 279 kcal (11g fat, 2g protein, 6g fiber)

Ingredients (6 servings)
1 tablespoon flour
1-quart water
1 chicken bouillon cube
1 1/2 tablespoons butter
12 garlic cloves, chopped
1/4 cup dry white wine
1/4 cup white vinegar
2 eggs
1 loaf bread, sliced
Salt, to taste
Black pepper, to taste

Preparation
Heat and melt the butter in a soup pot and add in the chopped garlic. Sauté until the garlic is golden, then add the flour, keep stirring. Pour in the chicken stock and cook this over medium-high heat for 10 minutes. Separate the two eggs. Blend the vinegar with egg yolks in the wine glass and pour this into the soup pot. Next, stir well. Add the dry white wine and mix well. Beat the whites and add to the soup pot. Cook for 5 minutes then serves warm.

Italian Buttery Onion Soup

Preparation time: 5 minutes
Cooking time: 30 minutes
Nutrition facts (per serving): 294 kcal (fats 23g, proteins 11g, fibers 1g)

Ingredients (6 servings)
2 cups of shredded mozzarella cheese
2 cups of milk
½ cup of cubed butter
¼ cup of flour
2 cups of thinly sliced onions
2 cups of chicken broth
Salt and pepper

Preparation
Sauté the onions with butter until tender. Stir in the flour. Add the broth and milk and cook on a medium heat. Add the cheese and stir continuously until it melts. Season with salt and pepper.

Turkish Highland Meadow Soup

Preparation Time: 17 minutes
Cooking Time: 15 minutes
Nutrition facts (per serving): 156 kcal

Ingredients (2 servings)
1/2 cup of rice or broken rice (or substitute with 1 cup of cooked plain rice)
3 cups of water
1 large egg yolk
2 cups of plain yogurt
2 tablespoons of all-purpose flour
2 tablespoons of butter or margarine
2 tablespoons of dried mint
1 cup of water
1 teaspoon of salt
A dash of white pepper
1 teaspoon of hot red pepper flakes

Preparation
In a large saucepan boil 3 cups of water. Add rice and cook until softened. While the rice is cooking, take a small mixing bowl, add the egg yolk, flour, yogurt and 1 cup of water and beat with a wire whisk until it turns into a creamy mixture with no lumps at all. When the rice is softened enough, whisk the water and rice mixture with a wire whisk and add in the creamy mixture. Add seasonings according to your taste. Whisk the mixture continuously and add more water if the mixture is thick.

In a separate pan, melt the butter, add in the dried mint and heat for 40 seconds. Remove from the heat quickly and add the butter and mint to the soup mixture. Mix well, cook for another minute and serve hot with a fresh mint garnish.

Vegetable Soup

Preparation Time: 25 minutes
Cooking Time: 20 minutes
Nutrition facts (per serving): 220 kcal

Ingredients (2 servings)
2 tablespoons of red lentil, washed
2 tablespoons of pearl barley
2 tablespoons of lemon juice
3 cups of water
1 cube of chicken bouillon
1 medium carrot, grated
1 medium potato, grated
1 small celery root, grated
Salt to taste

Preparation
In a large pan cook the water, lemon juice, barley and salt on medium heat. In the meantime, prepare all the vegetables and lentils. Add them into the pot. Cook until all the ingredients soften. Serve while hot.

Greek Lentil Soup

Preparation time: 15 minutes
Cook time: 20 minutes

Ingredients (4 servings)
3/4 cup brown lentils
1 large sliced onion
2 crushed cloves garlic
1 (3 ounce) can tomato purée
8 ounces fresh peeled and seeded tomatoes
Pinch of oregano
2 tablespoons olive oil
3 3/4 cups water
Salt and Pepper to taste

Preparation
Cover lentils with cold water and bring to boil. Drain lentils and return to the pan with garlic, onion, 1 1/2 pints water, tomato purée, fresh tomatoes, olive oil, and oregano. Bring to a boil and simmer until the lentils are soft. Remove from the heat and blend but stop blending before the mixture gets too smooth. Season to taste.

Main Dishes

Creole Rice Pilaf

Preparation time: 15 minutes
Cook time: 30 minutes
Nutrition facts (per serving): 249 kcal (3.6g fat, 2g protein, 5.4g fiber)

Ingredients (4 servings)
2 cups white long-grain rice
4 cups of water
1 cup fine egg noodles crushed
1 cup frozen peas
4 tablespoon salted butter
1 teaspoon meat magic
1 teaspoon black pepper

Preparation
Add the butter and egg noodles to a saucepan and sauté until golden. Pour in the water and mix well. Stir in the white rice, meat magic, peas, and black pepper then cook the mixture to a boil. Reduce its heat, cover, and cook on low heat for 20 minutes with occasional stirring. Garnish with paprika and red pepper flakes before serving.

Yogurt Pasta

Preparation time: 10 minutes
Cook time: 20 minutes
Nutrition facts (per serving): 326 kcal (17g fat, 4g protein, 1.2g fiber)

Ingredients (4 servings)
1/2-pound spaghetti
1-pound (500g) plain yogurt
1 tablespoon ghee
2 cloves mashed garlic
A pinch of paprika
Salt to taste
Roasted pine nuts
Chopped parsley

Preparation
Cook the spaghetti according to the package's instructions, drain, and set it aside. Beat the yogurt with salt in a bowl then stir in the spaghetti. Sauté the garlic with ghee in a pan for 2 minutes, then pour over the angel hair. Garnish with pine nuts and parsley and then serve.

Romanian Goulash

Preparation time: 30 minutes
Cooking time: 2 hours

Ingredients (8 servings)
8 tablespoon olive oil
4 medium onions
4 pounds stewing pork diced
8 tablespoon Hungarian paprika
2 pounds tomatoes, chopped
4 cloves garlic finely chopped
2 tablespoon tomato paste
8 tablespoon butter
2 carrots chopped
8 cups sauerkraut drained
6 bay leaves torn
2 bell peppers
8 tablespoon sour cream
4 tablespoon parsley chopped

Preparation
Warm the butter and olive oil to moderate heat in a large, heavy bottom pan with a lid. Add the garlic and onions. Sauté 4 minutes, until softened and then add the pork. Sauté until the pork is browned on all sides. Add the carrot, paprika, bell pepper and drained but not rinsed sauerkraut. Add bay leaves, tomato paste (puree) and tomatoes. Stir well to combine. Bring to a boil, then turn the heat to low and allow to simmer, covered for 65-70 minutes. Remove the lid and allow to simmer for an additional hour. Remove from the heat and stir in the sour cream. Serve over polenta, creamy mashed potatoes or pasta. Garnish with parsley.

Cabbage With Noodles

Preparation time: 10 minutes
Cooking time: 30 minutes
Nutritional Facts (per serving): 399 kcal (12 g protein, 8 g fat, 5 g fiber)

Ingredients (8 servings)
6 slices bacon thickly cut and chopped
6 tablespoons unsalted butter divided
2 large onions chopped
1 1/2 pounds cored green cabbage and cut into bite-sized pieces
1/2 teaspoons salt or to taste
1/4 teaspoons pepper or to taste
1 pound egg noodles of your choice, like penne or fusilli

Preparation
In a Dutch oven, fry the bacon until almost crispy. Add 3 tablespoons butter and melt. Add the onions and cook for 6 minutes or until soft and translucent. Add the cabbage, salt and pepper, stir everything together and cook, covered for 9-12 minutes until the cabbage has softened. Meanwhile, cook the noodles according to the instructions on the package. Drain and set aside. Add the cooked noodles to the Dutch oven together with the remaining 3 tablespoons butter and stir. Cook for a few more minutes until everything is heated through. Taste and season with salt and pepper if necessary.

Sweet Chicken With Cherry Sauce

Preparation Time: 2 minutes
Cooking Time: 20 minutes
Nutrition facts (per serving): 689 kcal

Ingredients (4 servings)
1 whole chicken
2 tablespoons of butter
1 lemon, cut in 4
1 small onion, peeled
1 teaspoon of oregano
Salt to taste
Pepper to taste

Cherry Sauce
1 cup of cherry compote juice, in a jar-in light syrup
1 1/2 cups of cherries
1 tablespoon of butter, unsalted
4 tablespoons of sugar
1 tablespoon of honey
1 teaspoon of cinnamon
1 tablespoon of corn starch
1 /4 cup of sliced almonds, roasted

Preparation
Wash the chicken and dry it with a paper towel. Season the inside and outside of the chicken with salt and pepper. Also season the inside with oregano and place the lemon wedges and onion in it. Spread the butter all over the chicken with your hand. Place the chicken in an oven dish, cover with aluminum foil. Preheat the oven and cook the prepared chicken for 28-32 minutes. Remove the aluminum foil; reduce the heat to 350 F and cook for another 60 minutes. Let the chicken sit for 12 minutes and then cut in four.

Cherry Sauce

Place the honey, sugar, cinnamon and corn starch in a small pot over medium heat. Slowly add 1 cup of cherry compote juice and stir constantly to avoid lumps. When it gets thicker, add in the cherries and butter. Cook for another minute and turn the heat off. Place the baked chicken pieces on serving plates. Pour the cherry sauce over the chicken, sprinkle some roasted almonds and serve.

Russian Chicken Shashlik In Nut Marinade

Preparation time: 15 minutes
Cooking time: 24 minutes
Nutrition facts (per serving): 428 kcal (fats 17g, proteins 57g, fibers 8g)

Ingredients (4 servings)
1 pound (500 g) of chicken breast
1 bunch of spring onions
2 garlic cloves, minced
½ lemon, juiced
1/2 cup (50 g) of ground nuts
2 tablespoons of olive oil
Salt and black pepper to taste

Preparation
Mix the green onion with ground nuts in a bowl. Stir the garlic and oil in, then mix well. Rub the chicken cubes with black pepper and salt. Add the chicken to the bowl and mix well. Cover and refrigerate for 30 minutes. Thread the chicken on the skewers. Set a grill over a medium heat and grease its grilling grates. Grill the skewers for 6 minutes per side until the chicken turns brown. Serve warm.

Steamed Salmon With Parsley Sauce

Preparation time: 15 minutes
Cooking time: 20 minutes
Nutrition facts (per serving): 442 kcal (fats 37g, proteins 21g, fibers 0g)

Ingredients (4 servings)
3 1/3 pounds (1,5kg) of salmon
3 ½ ounces (100 g) of butter
1 cup of dry white wine
1/2 cup of pickle brine
1 bunch of parsley, chopped
1 bay leaf
For the sauce
1 bunch of parsley
1 shallot, chopped
1/2 cup of dry white wine
1 cup of fish stock
7 ounces (270 g) of butter, cut into pieces
Salt and black pepper to taste

Preparation
Add the butter to a pan and place it on low heat. Stir the pickle brine, white wine, bay leaf and parsley in. Cook this mixture to a boil, then add the salmon pieces. Cover and cook on low heat for 10 minutes. Meanwhile, sauté the shallots in a pan with white wine. Pour the fish stock in and cook this mixture until reduced to half. Remove this pan from the heat. Add black pepper, salt and butter. Stir the parsley in and cook until the leaves have wilted. Top the salmon pieces with the parsley mixture. Serve warm.

Spicy Potato Quesadillas

Preparation time: 15 minutes
Cook time: 20 minutes

Ingredients (4 servings)
2 baked or boiled medium potatoes, coarsely mashed
4 (10-inch) flour tortillas
1 tablespoon olive oil
1/2 cup chopped onion
1 1/2 teaspoons chopped canned chipotle chili in adobo
Salt
Freshly ground black pepper

Preparation
In a large skillet, heat the oil over medium heat. Add the onion, cover, and cook until softened, about 6 minutes. Add the potatoes to the skillet and stir in the chipotle and salt and pepper to taste.

Spread a layer of the potato mixture evenly over each of the tortillas and fold them in half. Arrange two of the quesadillas in a large nonstick skillet or griddle over medium-heat and cook until lightly browned on both sides, turning once. Cut into quarters and serve warm.

Fast And Easy Pork Sausage

Preparation time: 15 minutes
Cooking time: 15 minutes
Nutritional Facts (per serving): 103 kcal (5 g protein, 3 g fat, 1 g fiber)

Ingredients (6 servings)
1 pound ground pork
2 cloves garlic finely chopped
2 tablespoons olive oil
1/2 teaspoon dried thyme
1 tablespoon fresh parsley chopped
1 teaspoons salt or to taste
1/4 cup breadcrumbs
1 large egg

Preparation
Add all ingredients except the olive oil to a large bowl and mix well everything. Divide the mixture into 12 equal portions and shape each portion into a sausage. Add the olive oil to a frying pan and heat over medium heat. Fry the sausages gently for 12 to 15 minutes until golden brown on all sides and cooked through.

Italian Grilled Shrimp Skewers

Preparation time: 10 minutes
Cooking time: 5 minutes
Nutritional Facts (per serving): 133 kcal (7g protein, 7g fat, 3g fiber)

Ingredients (9 servings)
3 tablespoons Italian parsley chopped
2 tablespoons lemon juice
18 large shrimp
18 zucchini slices
1/4 cup olive oil
1 clove garlic minced
1/4 teaspoon salt
2 teaspoons hot pepper flakes

Preparation
Soak 9 skewers in water for 30 minutes. In a small bowl, mix olive oil, lemon juice, chopped garlic, chopped Italian parsley, salt, and hot pepper flakes to combine. Cover and let stand at room temperature for 30 minutes. Once the 30 minutes have passed, heat the grill to a moderate-high heat.

Peel the shrimp and dry with a kitchen towel. Cut the zucchini into 1/4-inch slices. Alternate the shrimp and zucchini on the skewer. Brush the shrimp skewers with marinade and grill for about 3-5 minutes on each side or until the shrimp are cooked (pink on the outside, white and opaque on the inside). Baste regularly with the marinade while grilling. Brush with marinade again before serving.

Meatballs In Garlic Yogurt Sauce

Preparation Time: 35 minutes
Cooking Time: 10 minutes
Nutrition facts (per serving): 989 kcal

Ingredients (6 servings)
½ tablespoon of black peppercorns
6 cloves
¼ cup of roasted chickpeas
1 pound of beef mince
3 tablespoons of fried onions
4 green chilies, chopped
1 small onion, chopped
½ cup of fresh coriander
1 tablespoon of ground spices powder
¼ tablespoon of turmeric powder
1 tablespoon of ginger garlic paste
1 tablespoon of mustard oil
2 tablespoons of cooking oil
1 tablespoon of coriander powder
2 cups of yogurt
3 garlic cloves
Salt to taste
Red chili powder to taste

Preparation
In a spice mixer, add all the spices and roasted chickpeas and blend to make a fine powder. In a chopper, add the ground spices, beef mince, fried onions, green chilies, fresh onion, coriander, ground spices powder, salt, red chili powder, turmeric powder, ginger garlic paste and mustard oil and chop well. Wet your hands with oil, take 2 tablespoons of the mixture and make around 15 meatballs. Place the prepared meatballs in a pot. Cover and steam the meatballs

on a low flame for about 15 minutes. Keep turning so that they get golden all around. Add water, cover and cook on a low flame for 10 minutes. Add the cooking oil, coriander and turmeric powder, red chili powder and salt and mix well. Now in a small jug, add the yogurt, salt and garlic and whisk well. Serve with potato fries, garlic yogurt and fresh coriander.

Shrimp And Vegetable Clay Pot Casserole

Preparation Time: 20 minutes
Cooking Time: 15 minutes
Nutrition facts (per serving): 476 kcal

Ingredients (4 servings)
1 1/3 pounds of shrimps
1 tablespoon of tomato paste
2 green bell peppers
1 cup of small button mushrooms, fresh
3 Hungarian wax peppers
1 onion, chopped
3 garlic cloves, chopped
3 tablespoons of olive oil
3 ripe tomatoes
1 teaspoon of salt
¼ teaspoon of black pepper
¼ teaspoon of hot red pepper flakes
1 cup of grated yellow cheese

Preparation
Fill a medium saucepan with water. Add one teaspoon of salt, boil and add the shrimps. Boil for 2 minutes. Rinse the shrimps and run them in cold water. Clean and chop the green peppers. Clean the mushrooms. Fry the onions and garlic in a saucepan in the heated olive oil until they soften and become transparent. Add the green peppers. Add the chopped mushrooms, tomatoes, tomato paste and spices and stir until the mixture dries out. Add the cooked shrimps. Transfer the mixture to a large pot or an oven-proof dish. Generously cover with cheese. Cook the casserole in the oven, set until the cheese has melted, is bubbly and brown. Remove and immediately serve while it's still hot.

Cauliflower Stew

Preparation Time: 15 minutes
Cooking Time: 20 minutes
Nutrition facts (per serving): 97 kcal

Ingredients (4 servings)
1 medium-sized cauliflower, broken into florets
2 carrots, peeled and sliced
1 onion, peeled and sliced into half-moons
1 tablespoon of Turkish *salca*
2 tablespoons of tomato paste
1 tablespoon of olive oil
1 teaspoon of chili flakes or paprika
A handful of chopped flat leaf parsley
Salt and pepper to taste

Preparation
Heat the olive oil in a deep pan, add the onion and sauté until it starts to sweat or become transparent. Add your carrots and stir them around. Keep the flame low and gently sauté for 4-6 minutes, or until your carrot begins to cook and soften. Add salt, pepper or chili flakes. Meanwhile, put the tomato paste and *salca* into a cup and add boiling water or vegetable stock. Stir until the *salca* dissolves. Add the cauliflower to the pan along with the dissolved *salca*. Now add enough hot water or stock to cover the cauliflower florets. Stir everything, bring to a boil and then simmer until your cauliflower is soft. Top with chopped parsley.

Chicken Potato Stew

Preparation time: 10 minutes
Cooking time: 28 minutes
Nutrition facts (per serving): 408 kcal (fats 6.2g, proteins 34g, fibers 4g)

Ingredients (2 servings)
1 tablespoon of butter
1¼ pounds (540 g) of boneless chicken breast, cubed
5 potatoes, peeled and cubed
1 carrot, sliced
1 onion, chopped
1 tablespoon of tomato paste
1 pinch of salt and ground black pepper
2 cups of water to cover
1 bunch of fresh parsley, chopped

Preparation
Set a large saucepan over a medium heat. Add the butter to melt, then sear the chicken for 5 minutes per side. Stir in the carrots, potatoes and onions, then sauté for 8 minutes. Add the tomato paste, black pepper and salt, then add enough water to cover the chicken. Cook for 15 minutes on a simmer. Garnish with parsley. Serve warm.

Russian Piroshki

Preparation time: 15 minutes
Cooking time: 20 minutes
Nutrition facts (per serving): 184 kcal (fats 4.7g, proteins 20g, fibers 1.7g)

Ingredients (4 servings)
1 1/2 cups and 2 tablespoons of vegetable oil
2 cups of cabbage, thinly sliced
1/2 cup of onions, finely chopped
1/2-pound of ground beef
3/4 teaspoon of dried dill
1/2 teaspoon of garlic powder
3/4 teaspoon of salt
1/4 teaspoon of black pepper
1 (16 ounce/453 g) package of refrigerated biscuits

Preparation
Add 2 tablespoons of oil to a large skillet and place it over a medium heat. Stir the onions and cabbage in, then sauté for 7 minutes. Transfer the cabbage mixture to a bowl and keep it aside. Return the same skillet to a medium-high heat. Stir the beef in and sauté for 5 minutes until brown. Add the sautéed cabbage and black pepper, salt, garlic powder and dill.

Separate the biscuit in half to get 16 flat balls. Spread each ball into 3-inch circles. Top each circle with a tablespoon of meat mixture and fold them in half. Pinch the edges to seal the filling. Set a skillet over a medium-high heat. Add 1 ½ cups of oil to the skillet and heat to 350 degrees F. Fry the dumplings for 2 minutes per side until golden brown. Transfer the dumplings to a plate lined with a paper towel. Serve warm.

Mushroom Julienne

Preparation time: 15 minutes
Cooking time: 25 minutes
Nutrition facts (per serving): 273 kcal (fats 23g, proteins 8g, fibers 2g)

Ingredients (4 servings)
16 ounces (450 g) of white mushrooms, sliced
1/2 yellow onion, sliced
3 tablespoons of butter
1/4 cup of white wine
3/4 cup of sour cream
1/2 cup of heavy cream
Salt and black pepper, to taste
2 tablespoons of mozzarella cheese, shredded

Preparation
Preheat the oven to 375 degrees F. Add the mushrooms, onions and 2 tablespoons of butter to a pan. Sauté until the mushrooms are soft. Transfer the mushrooms to a casserole dish. Set a small pot over a medium heat. Add 1 tablespoon of butter and white wine to a pot. Cook this mixture for 1 minute. Stir the sour cream and heavy cream in. Add black pepper and salt. Boil this mixture and pour over the mushrooms. Sprinkle the cheese on top and bake for 10 minutes until it's melted.

Trout With Honey, Mustard and Lemon

Preparation time: 15 minutes
Cooking time: 15 minutes
Nutrition facts (per serving): 236 kcal (fats 13.8g, proteins 18g, fibers 1.7g)

Ingredients (2 servings)
2 trout, cut into fillets
1 tablespoon of honey
1 tablespoon of mustard
1 tablespoon of vegetable oil
1 lemon
Black pepper and salt to taste

Preparation
Clean and pat dry the trout. Mix the mustard, honey, oil, lemon juices and lemon zest in a bowl. Rub the trout with black pepper and salt. Place the fillets in a baking tray. Drizzle the marinade on top and marinate for 10 minutes. Set a grill on a medium-high heat and grease its grilling grates. Grill the fillets for 5 minutes per side until the fish is flaky and serve.

Tofu Crunchies

Preparation time: 10 minutes
Cook time: 25 minutes

Ingredients (7 servings)
1 pound extra-firm tofu, well drained and pressed
1 teaspoon Cajun seasoning
2 tablespoons olive oil
1/2 teaspoon salt
1/5 teaspoon freshly ground black pepper

Preparation
Preheat the oven to 350 F. Lightly oil a baking sheet and set aside. Cut the tofu slices into 1/4-inch strips. In a medium bowl, gently toss the tofu strips with the oil, salt, Cajun spice blend, and pepper, until well coated.

Arrange in a single layer on the prepared baking sheet, and bake 43-47 minutes or until nicely browned, turning once with a metal spatula about halfway through. Set aside to let them cool before serving.

Bulgur Wheat Pilaf

Preparation time: 10 minutes
Cook time: 20 minutes
Nutrition facts (per serving): 367 kcal (6g fat, 9g protein, 1.2g fiber)

Ingredients (4 servings)
2 cups *Bulgur*
3 tablespoons canola oil
2 1/2 cups water
Salt to taste

Preparation
Add the *Bulgur* and all the ingredients to a cooking pot and cook until the water is completely absorbed. Stir the *bulgur* after every 10 minutes. Serve warm.

Vegan Margherita Pizza

Preparation time: 15 minutes
Cook time: 25 minutes

Ingredients (4 servings)
2 ripe plum tomatoes, sliced paper thin
1 1/2 tablespoons olive oil
1/4 cup vegan basil pesto, homemade
1 recipe basic pizza dough
1 cup drained firm tofu
1 tablespoon nutritional yeast
Salt and freshly ground black pepper

Preparation
Preheat the oven to 450 F. Flatten the risen dough slightly, cover with plastic wrap or a clean towel, and set aside to relax for 12 minutes. Place the oven rack on the lowest level of the oven. Lightly oil a pizza pan or large baking sheet. Turn the relaxed dough onto a lightly floured surface and flatten with your hands, turning and flouring frequently, working it into a 12-inch round. Don't overwork the middle or the center of the crust will be too thin. Transfer the dough to the prepared pizza pan or baking sheet.

In a food processor, combine the nutritional yeast and tofu and process until smooth. Add salt and pepper and blend until smooth. Set aside. Blot any excess liquid from the tomato slices with paper towels. Spread 1/2 tablespoon of the olive oil onto the prepared pizza dough, using your fingertips to spread evenly. Top with the tofu mixture, spreading evenly to about 1/2 inch from the dough's edge. Whisk the remaining 1 tablespoon of oil into the pesto and spread evenly over the tofu mixture to about 1/2 inch from the dough's edge. Arrange the tomato slices on the pizza and season with salt and pepper to taste. Bake 11-13 minutes, until the crust is golden brown.

Hummus Pasta With Orange

Preparation time: 5 minutes
Cook time: 10 minutes

Ingredients

2.5 oz of spaghetti or pasta of your choice
1 zucchini, spiralized
2 cups of baby spinach or kale
1/4 cup hummus
1 orange

Preparation

Bring a saucepan of salted water to a boil and cook the pasta. When the pasta is fully cooked, add the zoodles and greens for 30 seconds, but not more (learn from my mistakes). Scoop out about half a cup of cooking water and set aside. Drain the pasta and vegetables and return to the saucepan. Add the hummus, a squeeze of orange, salt, pepper, and a little splash of cooking water. Toss everything together until combined and well coated with hummus and serve.

Pasta Tomatina

Preparation time: 15 minutes
Cooking time: 20 minutes

Ingredients (6 servings)

2 pounds whole wheat pasta
2 medium carrot diced
2 medium onion diced
6 cloves garlic minced
3 teaspoon maple syrup
2 pinch red pepper flakes
2 clove garlic sliced
2 28 oz. can whole tomatoes
2 teaspoon dried basil
15 fresh leaves fresh basil julienned
Sea salt and pepper to taste

Preparation

Sauté the onion in about 1/3 cup water for a few minutes. Add the minced garlic, carrots, and continue to cook until translucent and soft. Add the dried basil, red pepper flakes, and whole tomatoes, using your hands to crush or an immersion blender. Add the maple syrup and salt and pepper. Bring to a boil, reduce heat to a simmer and cook partially covered for about 22 minutes. Add fresh basil and stir. Taste to see if you need more seasonings. Cook the pasta according to the package directions. Drain and add pasta to the pan and toss to coat with the sauce. Add extra basil to the plated pasta, if desired, with a few slices of garlic.

Spicy Potato Curry

Preparation time: 10 minutes
Cook time: 30 minutes

Ingredients

4 potatoes, peeled and cubed
2 tablespoons vegetable oil
1 yellow onion, diced
3 cloves garlic, minced
2 teaspoons ground cumin
1 1/2 teaspoons cayenne pepper
4 teaspoons curry powder
4 teaspoons garam masala
1 (1 inch) piece fresh ginger root, peeled and minced
2 teaspoons salt
1 (14.5 ounce) can diced tomatoes
1 (15 ounce) can chickpeas, rinsed and drained 1 (15 ounce) can peas, drained 1 (14 ounce) can coconut milk

Preparation

Place potatoes into a large pot and cover with salted water. Bring to a boil over high heat, then reduce heat to medium-low, cover, and simmer 14-16 minutes or until just tender. Drain and allow to steam dry for 2 minutes.

Heat the vegetable oil in a large skillet over medium heat. Stir in the garlic and onion. Cook and stir about 5 minutes or until the onion has softened and turned translucent. Season with curry powder, garam masala, cumin, cayenne pepper, ginger, and salt and cook for 3 minutes more. Add the potatoes, tomatoes, chickpeas, and peas. Pour in the coconut milk and bring to a simmer. Simmer 8-11 minutes before serving.

Chicken Thighs With Lemon

Preparation time: 5 minutes
Cook time: 30 minutes
Nutrition facts (per serving): 564 kcal (50g protein, 32g fat, 11g carbs)

Ingredients (4 ingredients)
8 chicken thighs
2 tablespoon olive oil
1 garlic clove
2 tablespoon lemon juice
A pinch of salt and pepper

Preparation
Heat a pan on the medium heat and add a tablespoon lemon juice and the minced garlic clove. Stir for 2 minutes. Take a bowl, put the chicken thighs in it, and add the remaining lemon, salt and pepper. Mix it well. Put the chicken thighs onto the heated pan and lower the heat. Cook for 30 minutes and serve.

Chicken Piccata

Preparation time: 15 minutes
Cook time: 20 minutes
Nutrition facts (per serving): 244 kcal (6g fat, 28g protein, 1.5g fiber)

Ingredients (6 servings)

3 chicken breast fillets, halved horizontally
3 1/2 ounces butter, chopped
1/4 cup drained baby capers
3 lemons, zested, juiced
1/2 cup flat-leaf parsley, chopped

Preparation

Place each boneless chicken fillet between 2 sheets of plastic wrap. Use a mallet to gently pound until into 2/3 inch thick fillet. Heat 1 ½ tablespoon butter in a large non-stick skillet over high heat. Sear the chicken, in batches, for 2 minutes each side until golden. Transfer to a suitable plate and cover with a loose foil. Reduce the heat to medium then the remaining butter to the pan. Cook for 3 minutes until butter is golden brown. Stir in the capers and cook for 1 minute until crispy. Stir in lemon juice and half the lemon zest. Swirl to combine. Return the cooked and sear chicken and its juices to the pan. Sauté, for 2 minutes until the chicken is cooked through and sauce thickens. Garnish with parsley and any remaining lemon zest. Serve warm.

Quick Stew

Preparation time: 5 minutes
Cook time: 30 minutes

Ingredients
1 onion, chopped
3 carrots, chopped
3 potatoes, chopped
1 parsnip, chopped
1 turnip, chopped
1/4 cup uncooked white rice
1 teaspoon ground black pepper
1 teaspoon ground cumin
1 teaspoon salt
2 1/2 cups water

Preparation
In a large pot over medium-high heat, combine potatoes, onion, carrots, parsnip, turnip, rice, cumin, pepper, salt and water. Boil 28-32 minutes or until vegetables are tender, adding more water, if necessary.

Syrian Mejaddarah

Preparation time: 15 minutes
Cook time: 21 minutes
Nutrition facts (per serving): 273 kcal (13g fat, 8g protein, 2g fiber)

Ingredients (4 servings)
2 cup white rice
1/2 cup boiled brown lentils
2 onion chopped slides
1/4 cup vegetable oil
3 cup hot water
2 cubes of chicken stock
1 pinch salt

Preparation
Add vegetable oil, lentils, and rice to a saucepan then stir cook for 1 minute. Pour in 3 cups water, chicken stock, and salt then cover to cook for 20 minutes on low heat. Meanwhile, sauté the onion with oil in a separate pan until golden brown. Add the onions on top of the rice and serve warm.

Sautéed Broad Beans

Preparation time: 10 minutes
Cook time: 15 minutes
Nutrition facts (per serving): 278 kcal (11g fat, 5g protein, 3g fiber)

Ingredients (6 servings)
2 pounds (1 kg) broad beans
2 ounces (70 ml) olive oil
6 garlic cloves, minced
3 1/2 ounces (100 g) fresh coriander, chopped
¼ teaspoon salt
Juice of 1 lemon
9 ounces (250 g) yogurt
Arabic pita bread

Preparation
Add the broad beans to a cooking pot and pour enough water to cover the beans. Cook for 5 minutes. Drain and transfer to an ice-water. Push the beans out of their skins. Sauté garlic and coriander with olive oil in a pan on low heat until brown. Stir in the beans, lemon juice, and mix well. Serve warm.

Rice With Pomegranate

Preparation time: 10 minutes
Cook time: 30 minutes
Nutrition facts (per serving): 657 kcal (42g protein, 54g fat, 98g carbs)

Ingredients (4 servings)
2 cups rice
2 pounds beef
½ cup olive oil
1 pomegranate
3 onions
Salt and pepper to taste

Preparation
Squeeze the pomegranate and set it aside. Cut the beef in thin slices, put in the pan, add 5 tablespoon olive oil, and cook on the medium heat for 12 minutes. After 12 minutes add pomegranate juice and diced onions. In meanwhile take a saucepan, add 4 cups of water and 2 cups of rice, the remaining of olive oil and a pinch of salt. Cook the rice for 30 minutes on the medium heat and serve.

Chicken Breast Ragout With Mushrooms

Preparation time: 10 minutes
Cook time: 30 minutes
Nutrition facts (per serving): 438 kcal (46g protein, 22g fat, 21g carbs)

Ingredients (4 servings)
1 red pepper
1 green pepper
2 tomatoes
1 pound of chicken breast
1 cup mushrooms
½ pound tomato sauce
1 onion
½ cup basmati rice
4 tablespoon olive oil

Preparation
Cut into slices the green and red peppers, tomatoes, mushrooms, and the chicken breast. In a pan, add 2 tablespoon of olive oil, sliced green and red peppers, diced tomatoes, and stir them well for 5 minutes. Add the sliced mushrooms and cook for another 3 minutes. Put another pan on the low heat, add a tablespoon of olive oil and pour in the sliced chicken breast.

Cook the chicken for 15-20 minutes; and after that, mix with the green and red pepper combination. Meanwhile, take a saucepan, and cook the rice with a cup of water and olive oil on the medium heat for 20 minutes. Finally, for serving, put the rice and top it with the chicken breast mixture.

Fish Pie

Preparation time: 15 minutes
Cooking time: 30 minutes
Nutrition facts (per serving): 343 kcal (fats 23g, proteins 13g, fibers 0.6g)

Ingredients (6 servings)

2 teaspoons of butter
1 (8 ounce/230 g) container of sour cream
½ teaspoon of baking soda
1 cup and 3 tablespoons of all-purpose flour
3 large eggs
½ cup of mayonnaise
1 teaspoon of salt
1 (6 ½ ounce/220 g) can of salmon, drained and flaked

Preparation

Preheat the oven to 400 degrees F. Grease an iron skillet. Whisk the sour cream with baking soda in a large bowl. Beat the eggs in another bowl. Stir 3 tablespoons of flour, salt and mayonnaise in. Mix well until it makes a smooth and lump-free batter. Spread half of this batter on the greased pie plate. Add the fish on top of the batter and pour the remaining batter on top. Bake for 30 minutes in the preheated oven. Serve warm.

Russian Beef With Veggies

Preparation time: 10 minutes
Cooking time: 15 minutes
Nutrition facts (per serving): 478 kcal (fats 11g, proteins 55g, fibers 3g)

Ingredients (4 servings)
2 slices of white bread
1/2 cup of milk
1 medium onion, peeled and grated
12 ounces (340 g) of ground pork
12 ounces (340 g) of ground beef
1 1/2 teaspoons of salt
1/2 teaspoon of black pepper
1 1/2 cups of breadcrumbs
1 cup of vegetable oil, for frying

Preparation
Soak the bread in milk and then transfer to a large bowl. Stir the meats, salt, black pepper and onions in. Mix well and make golf ball sized meatballs out of this mixture. Press the meatballs into cutlets. Coat the cutlets with breadcrumbs and leave them for 10 minutes. In a large skillet, heat oil for deep frying. Add the cutlets to the oil and cook for 5 minutes per side until golden brown. Serve warm.

Shrimp Pan With Parsley, Lemon, and Garlic

Preparation time: 25 minutes
Cook time: 20 minutes
Nutrition fact (per serving): 182 kcal (1 oz. protein, ¼ oz. fat)

Ingredients (4 servings)
28 oz. raw shrimp (1 oz. each; headless, in shell)
4 garlic cloves
1 untreated lemon
2 tablespoon olive oil
1 bunch parsley
Salt and pepper to taste

Preparation
Wash the shrimp and pat dry. Peel and slice the garlic. Wash lemon with hot water, rub dry, and cut into slices. Heat oil in a pan. Fry the shrimp for 7-9 minutes while turning. After 3 minutes, add the garlic and lemon and fry. Wash the parsley, shake dry, pluck the leaves from the stalks and roughly chop. Season the shrimp with salt and pepper. Add parsley and stir in. Serve with toasted bread.

Cashew Zoodles

Preparation time: 10 minutes
Cook time: 10 minutes

Ingredients (2 servings)
2 medium zucchinis
1 tablespoon fresh cilantro chopped
2 large carrots peeled
3/4 cup cashews

Sauce
Juice of 1/2 lime
3 cloves garlic minced
2 heaping tablespoons peanut butter
1/2 tablespoon hoisin sauce
3/4 tablespoon sriracha sauce
1 teaspoon soy sauce

Preparation
Spiralize the carrots on the thinnest and the zucchini on the medium setting. Set aside. Add the sriracha sauce, peanut butter, hoisin sauce, soy sauce, lime juice, and garlic to a skillet on medium-high heat. Stirring constantly, cook it for 1-3 minutes or until the garlic has just started to cook. Add the carrots, cashews and zucchini. Using tongs or two large spoons, gently lift up the pan contents every 20 seconds or so for 5 minutes until everything is lightly cooked and heated through. The zucchini will release some liquid, which will help to make a nice sauce. Add the cilantro in and toss at the end to serve.

Spanish Chicken Pan

Preparation time: 20 minutes
Cook time: 20 minutes
Nutrition fact (per serving): 432 kcal (1 ½ oz. protein, 20 oz. fat, ½ oz. of carbohydrates)

Ingredients (4 servings)

4 onions
2 garlic cloves
6 beefsteak tomatoes
4 chicken fillets
3 tablespoon olive oil
2 oz. almond kernels
1 ¼ cups dry white wine
Salt and pepper to taste
½ bunch flat-leaf parsley
3 1/2 oz. black olives (without pits)

Preparation

Peel and finely dice onions and garlic. Wash tomatoes, roughly dice. Wash the meat, pat dry. Warm up the oven (electric stove: 350 ° F / convection: 300 ° F). Heat oil in a pan and fry the fillets on each side for 4-5 minutes. Place in an ovenproof dish and finish cooking in the hot oven for 9-11 minutes.

Briefly toast the almonds in the frying fat. Sauté the onions, garlic, and tomatoes. Deglaze with wine and season with salt and pepper. Simmer for 6–8 minutes. Wash and roughly chop parsley. Add to the vegetables with olives.

French Pilaf With Mushrooms

Preparation time: 20 minutes
Cook time: 20 minutes

Ingredients (4 servings)
5 oz mushrooms sliced
½ cup sun-dried tomatoes soaked in hot water and sliced
1 cup quinoa
1 cup low-sodium vegetable broth
1 cup frozen green peas
1/5 cup slivered almonds
sea salt and pepper to taste

Preparation
Sauté the mushrooms in a large pan over medium heat with very small amount of vegetable broth until cooked through. Add the quinoa, vegetable broth or water to the pan and heat until boiling. Turn down heat to simmer and cook 14-16 minutes until all of the water is absorbed. Add the peas during the last few minutes of cooking along with the sun-dried tomatoes, and slivered almonds. Stir to combine. Mix the dressing ingredients and add to the quinoa, mixing to combine.

Caucasus Beef Kebab

Preparation time: 10 minutes
Cook time: 22 minutes
Nutrition facts (per serving): 374 kcal (30g protein, 33g fat, 13g carbs)

Ingredients (6 servings)

7 oz onion
2 pounds minced beef
10 teaspoon olive oil
5 garlic cloves
Salt and pepper to taste

Preparation

Take a big bowl and add the minced beef. Mince the onion and garlic cloves and add to the beef. Add salt and pepper and mix it well, so that you get a smooth consistency. Take a handful of the mixture and make ellipse-shaped meatballs. Preheat a pan on the medium heat, add there the olive oil. Put the meatballs into the pan and cook for 5 minutes on each side. Total cooking time should be around 22 minutes.

Spanish Pepper Noodle Pan

Preparation time: 10 minutes
Cook time: 30 minutes
Nutrition fact (per serving): 570 kcal (30 oz. protein, 28 oz. fat, 33 oz. of carbohydrates)

Ingredients (5 servings)
18 oz. thrown pork neck (piece)
7 oz. Cabanossi
22 oz. tomatoes
3 bell peppers
1 onion
1 garlic clove
1 tablespoon Almond kernels (skinless)
2 tablespoons oil
9 oz. spaghettini
½ bunch of basil
Salt and pepper to taste

Preparation
Pat the meat dry and roughly dice. Cut the cabanossi into slices. Clean, wash and chop tomatoes and peppers. Peel and thinly dice the onion and garlic. If necessary, roughly chop the almonds. Heat the oil in a large stew pan. Fry the meat vigorously all around. Fry the Cabanossi briefly. Sauté the onion, garlic, paprika, and almonds for about 3 minutes. Spice up. Add tomatoes and ¾ cups water, simmer for 11-13 minutes. Break the pasta into pieces. Pour into the pan, stir in. Simmer for another 10 minutes. Stir every now and then, possibly adding some more hot water. Season the pasta pan to taste. Wash and pluck the basil, sprinkle over it.

Salmon With Tarragon Leaves

Preparation time: 5 minutes
Cook time: 20 minutes
Nutrition facts (per serving): 475 kcal (36g protein, 10.2g fat, 27g carbs)

Ingredients (2 servings)
1 salmon
¼ cup water
Sea salt to taste
Tarragon branch to taste

Preparation
Rinse and clean the salmon well. Next, salt, put in a saucepan, pour in a little water, and simmer on low heat for 16 minutes. Remove the saucepan from the fire, carefully transfer the salmon to a dish, cover with a damp cloth and store in a cool place until serving. When serving, garnish the fish with tarragon branches.

Baba Ganouj

Preparation time: 15 minutes
Cook time: 20 minutes
Nutrition facts (per serving): 212 kcal (9g fat, 17g protein, 0.5g fiber)

Ingredients (6 servings)
1 big eggplant, peeled and sliced
1 medium tomato, chopped
1/2 cup packed parsley, chopped
2 or 3 tablespoons pomegranate concentrate
1/3 cup pomegranate seeds
2 cloves mashed garlic
A dash of cumin
2 tablespoons olive oil
Salt and black pepper to taste

Preparation
Brush the eggplant slices with oil in a baking pan lined with aluminum foil. Roast the slices for 20 minutes at 350 degrees F until soft. Cut the eggplants into chunks. Blend the eggplant in a blender. Add parsley, garlic, spices, pomegranate concentrate, and salt then blend for 1 minute. Stir in the tomato, pomegranate seeds, and olive oil.

Zucchini Tomato Stew

Preparation time: 15 minutes
Cook time: 20 minutes
Nutrition facts (per serving): 356 kcal (15g fat, 26g protein, 0.7g fiber)

Ingredients (4 servings)

1-pound (500 g) chopped zucchini
14 ounces diced tomato
1/2-pound ground beef
1 clove mashed garlic
1 chopped medium onion
1 tablespoon lemon juice
2 tablespoon canola oil
1 teaspoon crushed mint
1/2 teaspoon *Bharat* (Syrian Spice Mix)
Salt and black pepper, to taste

Preparation

Sauté the onion with oil in a cooking pan until soft. Stir in beef and sauté until brown. Season it with black pepper and salt. Stir in the zucchini and cook for 3 minutes. Stir in the garlic, spices, salt, tomato, and mint. Cook the mixture to a boil then reduce the heat. Cook the stew for 15 minutes on simmer.

Spanish Potatoes

Preparation time: 15 minutes
Cook time: 20 minutes
Nutrition fact (per serving): 430 kcal (10 oz. protein, 1 ounce of fat, 40 oz. of carbohydrates)

Ingredients (4 servings)
2 lbs. of potatoes
1 red and green pepper
1 onion
1 garlic clove
1 teaspoon cumin
3 tablespoons of olive oil
12 slices Serrano ham
2 teaspoons of sweet paprika
2 tablespoons of sherry vinegar
Salt and chili pepper to taste
Parsley

Preparation
Wash the potatoes and boil for 18-22 minutes. Clean and wash the peppers and cut them into cubes. Peel and dice the onion. Peel and roughly chop the garlic. Finely crush the garlic and cumin in a mortar. Stir in 2 tablespoons of oil, paprika, and vinegar. Season to taste with salt and chili. Drain, rinse, peel, and cut the potatoes. Heat 3 tablespoons of oil in a pan and fry the potatoes in it. Add the onion and bell pepper and fry for about 5 minutes. Add the garlic mixture to the potatoes. Season again with salt and pepper. Garnish the potatoes with parsley and serve with ham.

Gambas In Garlic Oil

Preparation time: 10 minutes
Cook time: 15 minutes
Nutrition fact (per serving): 242 kcal (40 oz. protein, ½ oz. fat, ½ oz. of carbohydrates)

Ingredients (4 servings)
20 frozen prawns
4 garlic cloves
Salt and pepper to taste
6 tablespoons of olive oil

Preparation
Thaw the prawns at room temperature. Peel the garlic and cut into thin layers. Peel the prawns, except for the tail fin, and remove the intestines. Wash the prawns and pat dry. Season with salt and pepper. Heat oil in a pan. Fry the prawns, turning, for approximately 5-8 minutes. Add the garlic and fry. Arrange in a bowl.

Manchego Balls With Paprika Salsa

Preparation time: 10 minutes
Cook time: 20 minutes
Nutrition fact (per serving): 373 kcal (1 oz. protein, 20 oz. fat, ½ oz. of carbohydrates)

Ingredients (6 servings)
2 red and yellow peppers
2 spring onions
1 tablespoon lemon juice
1 tablespoon olive oil
1 slice toast
2 tablespoon flour
1 egg
3 tablespoon whipping cream
14 oz. Manchego cheese
Salt and Pepper to taste

Preparation
Quarter the peppers, clean, wash, pat dry, and finely dice. Wash the spring onions, pat dry and cut into fine rings. Season the lemon juice with salt, pepper, and sugar. Beat in the oil drop by drop. Mix the peppers, spring onions, and vinaigrette together. Cut bread into pieces and grind in the universal chopper. Mix the flour and breadcrumbs. Stir the egg and 2 tablespoons of heavy cream, season with a little salt and pepper.

Dice Manchego cheese turn first in egg, then in the flour mixture, and press down. Heat the frying oil. Fry the cheese in portions until golden brown, remove, and allow to drain on kitchen paper. Arrange the paprika salsa and cheese on small plates.

Armenian Johob

Preparation time: 10 minutes
Cook time: 30 minutes
Nutrition facts (per serving): 616 kcal (18g protein, 42g fat, 82g carbs)

Ingredients (4 servings)
2 pounds onion
3 pounds chicken
7 oz butter
20 oz pomegranate seeds
Seasoning to taste

Preparation
Chop the chicken into small pieces. Melt the butter in a pan and fry the chicken for 16 minutes or until half cooked. Add the onion chopped in half rings and fry for another 15 minutes on low heat. Add the pomegranate seeds and simmer for a while until the grains turn white.

Chicken Apricots Stir Fry

Preparation time: 5 minutes
Cook time: 20 minutes
Nutrition facts (per serving): 225 kcal (carbs 14 g, Fat 6 g, Protein 27 g)

Ingredients (4 servings)
1 pound chicken breast, cut into 2 inch cubes
4 large portabella mushrooms, cut into 2-inch cubes
4 oz dried apricots, coarsely chopped
1 cup cashews
¾ cup raisins
½ cup chicken broth
1 tablespoon brown sugar
2 teaspoons sweet paprika
½ teaspoon ground ginger
Oil
Salt and pepper

Preparation
Place a large pan over medium heat and heat a splash of oil in it. Add the chicken and brown it for 5-7 minutes and then add the mushrooms. Stir and cook them for 3 minutes. Stir in the apricots, brown sugar, raisins, paprika, ginger, and salt and pepper. Cook for 4-6 minutes. Stir in the broth and cook them for 7 minutes over high heat. Fold in the cashews.

Beetroot Pasta

Preparation time: 10 minutes
Cook time: 30 minutes
Nutrition facts (per serving): 218 kcal (7g protein, 3,1g fat, 42g carbs)

Ingredients (4 servings)

8 ½ oz spaghetti
8 oz beetroot
¼ cup dry white wine
1 teaspoon olive oil
1 onion
2 tablespoon nutmeg
2 ½ cup cups water

Preparation

Cut the beetroot into thin strips and chop the onion finely. Fry the beets with strips and then season with salt and pepper to taste before adding wine. Cook spaghetti in salted 2 ½ cups of water for 20 minutes, recline, cool, and fry in oil. To prevent the pasta from sticking to the pan, add some water. Mix the beet strips with spaghetti. Bring to a boil together, then add salt and pepper again. Lastly, sprinkle with nutmeg and serve.

Lime And Herby Baked Fish

Preparation time: 10 minutes
Cook time: 25 minutes
Nutrition facts (per serving): 419 kcal (carbs 18 g, Fat 11.2g, Protein 18g)

Ingredients (2 servings)
2 whole fish
1 teaspoon parsley, chopped
1 teaspoon thyme, chopped
1 teaspoon rosemary sprigs
1 lime, cut into thin slices
2 tablespoon lime juice
2 tablespoon honey
1 teaspoon chili flakes
6-8 peppercorns
2 tablespoon olive oil
Black pepper to taste
Salt to taste

Preparation
Clean the fish and cut a few slits on the skin. Next, add to a baking tray. Add lime slices onto the slit areas of the fish and around the fish, too. Add the peppercorns and herbs around the fish. Add olive oil, salt, pepper, chili flakes, honey, and lime juice on top. Bake for 20 minutes. Lastly, let it rest for 10 minutes before serving.

Persian Herbed Frittatas

Preparation time: 10 minutes
Cook time: 45 minutes
Nutrition facts (per serving): 523 kcal (carbs 20 g, Fat 10g, Protein 31g)

Ingredients (10 servings)

2 oz cilantro leaves, finely chopped
12 eggs, beaten
2 tablespoons olive oil (set more aside for greasing)
2 teaspoon flour
2 bunches scallions, chopped
1 teaspoon baking powder
2 tablespoons crumbled, dried fenugreek leaves
6 oz parsley, chopped
Ground black pepper
Salt

Preparation

Preheat oven to 375 F. Pour olive oil inside a skillet and heat over medium-high. Put parsley, scallions, and cilantro. Cook and stir constantly for about 6 minutes, just enough time until the content starts to droop. Take the skillet off the heat and leave the content to cool a little. While this is going on, grab a 12-cup muffin and grease with the oil. Break the eggs into a bowl and beat; add flour, baking powder, fenugreek leaves, salt, and pepper to season and taste. Go back to the herbs in the skillet and pour them into the egg mixture. Divide the mixture among the muffin cups. Leave to bake for 20-25 minutes until get the eggs to puff and color change to golden. Remove the muffin tin from the oven afterward and put on a rack. Let cool and then serve.

Chicken With Saffron

Preparation time: 10 minutes
Cook time: 30 minutes
Nutrition facts (per serving): 564 kcal (carbs 26 g, Fat 20g, Protein 40g)

Ingredients (6 servings)
6 chicken thighs
2 diced onions
1 tablespoon curry
Salt and pepper to taste
1 tablespoon olive oil
¾ cup chopped dates
3 tablespoons lemon juice
½ teaspoon saffron
1 diced fresh tomato

Preparation
Add the chicken and 1 onion to a pot. Season with salt, pepper, and curry. Cover the chicken with water and cover the pot and simmer for 11-12 minutes. Heat the olive oil. Fry the remaining onion for 5 minutes. Set aside. Transfer the chicken in the same skillet and fry for 9-11 minutes. Keep the water. Add the chopped dates to the skillet. Use a cup of the reserved "chicken water" and stir in the saffron and lemon juice. Pour the liquid into the skillet. Add the diced tomato and cover your skillet and simmer for 12 minutes.

Stew With Potato And Rice

Preparation time: 10 minutes
Cook time: 30 minutes
Nutrition facts (per serving): 260 kcal (Carbs 46 g, Fat 6g, Protein 4 g)

Ingredients (6 servings)

3 cups white long grain rice
¼ cup oil
4 potatoes
4 oz. water

Preparation

Place in it the rice in a larger bowl and cover it with hot water and a pinch of salt. Place it aside. Peel of the potato and slice them. Place a medium pot and fill ½ of it with water. Place in it the rice and cook it to boiling. Once the rice is half done, drain it.

Place a large pot over medium heat and heat the oil in it. Spread the potato in the pot and sprinkle on it some salt. Top it with rice. Make a hole in the center of the rice layer and another 4 holes on the side. Drizzle some water on top. Put on the lid and cook them for 3 min over high heat. Lower the heat and drizzle some oil top. Lower the heat to medium heat and cook it for 14-17 min and then further lower the heat to medium low. Drizzle more of some oil on top. Finally, cook it for 12 minutes and serve warm.

Salads

Zucchini Orzo Salad

Preparation time: 15 minutes
Cooking time: 15 minutes
Nutrition facts (per serving): 236 kcal (fats 5.6g, proteins 7.7g, fibers 2.3g)

Ingredients (4 servings)
2 zucchinis, quartered lengthwise and sliced
1 cup of orzo
4 teaspoons of olive oil
1 garlic clove, chopped
1 tablespoon of white wine
½ cup of fresh basil leaves
Salt and ground pepper

Preparation
Cook the orzo in salted boiling water until cooked through and drain. Spread them on a baking sheet and cool. Cook the zucchini in 1 tablespoon of hot oil until tender and season with salt and pepper. Mix the vinegar, orzo, basil, 1 tablespoon of oil and orzo in a bowl and cover using a wrap. Refrigerate for an hour before serving.

Twirls Salad

Preparation time: 15 minutes

Ingredients (4 servings)
1 (12 ounce) package uncooked rainbow twirled macaroni
1 cup crumbled feta, Roquefort or blue cheese
1/2 cup chopped black olives
3/4 cup sliced radishes
1/4 cup sliced scallion
1 cup marinated artichoke hearts
1/2 cup olive or vegetable oil
2 tablespoons lemon juice
2 tablespoons chopped fresh parsley
1 clove garlic, minced
1 teaspoon oregano

Preparation
Cook macaroni according to the package directions and drain. In a large bowl, toss the hot cooked twirls with olives, radishes, cheese, scallions, and artichoke hearts until well blended. In a small bowl, combine remaining ingredients. Toss with the twirl mixture until evenly coated. Salt and pepper to taste and chill.

Greek Hot Potato Salad

Preparation time: 15 minutes

Ingredients (4 servings)
5 large potatoes
1 sliced large onion
1/2 cup diced celery
1/2 cup olive oil
Chopped Parsley
Juice of 2 lemons
Salt and pepper

Preparation
Boil the potatoes until tender and keep hot. Slice the onion into a large bowl. Sprinkle with salt and cold water and allow to stand about 5 minutes, then drain. Slice the hot potatoes and add to the onions. Add celery, lemon juice, and olive oil. Mix well to absorb the dressing. Season to taste, and garnish with chopped parsley. Serve warm.

Mushroom Salad

Preparation time: 10 minutes
Cook time: 5 minutes
Nutrition facts (per serving): 136 kcal (5g protein, 7g fat, 12g carbs)

Ingredients (4 servings)
8 oz mushrooms
8 ½ oz sweet pepper
¼ cup bacon
½ cup celery root
4 tablespoon chopped parsley
1 tablespoon vegetable oil
Salt and ground black pepper to taste

Preparation
Cut the bacon into small cubes and the mushrooms into slices. Put a pan onto the fire with 2 tablespoon of olive oil. After 2 minutes, reduce the fire, add the mushrooms, and fry them for another 3 minutes. Sprinkle the mushrooms with herbs, mix, remove from heat and cool. Chop the pepper and celery into strips, combine, season with oil, salt, pepper, and mix well. Place the vegetables on the dish and lay the fried mushrooms on top.

Carrots Sauté

Preparation time: 5 minutes
Cooking time: 15 minutes

Ingredients
Carrots sliced thin (1/2 inch) like wheels
1 minced clove garlic
1 minced large onion
Oregano
Lemon juice
Olive oil
Salt, pepper

Preparation
Parboil (or microwave) the carrots for 5 minutes. Sauté the garlic and onion in olive oil. Add salt, pepper, lemon juice, and oregano. Put a lid on the frying pan and let it braise for 7 – 11 minutes.

Pomegranate Orange And Baby Spinach Salad

Preparation time: 10 minutes

Ingredients (4 servings)
2 handfuls baby spinach
½ seeded pomegranate
2 teaspoon pomegranate juice
1 orange in separated segments
Juice of 1 orange
½ teaspoon caster sugar

Preparation
Place the washed baby spinach on a plate. Mix the juice of half the orange with sugar and the pomegranate juice for dressing. Place the orange segments and pomegranate seeds on the spinach. Pour the dressing over the salad.

Carrot And Orange Salad

Preparation time: 15 minutes

Ingredients (4 servings)
1 pound shredded carrots
1/4 cup chopped fresh cilantro
2 tablespoons fresh orange juice
2 oranges, peeled, segmented, and chopped
1/2 cup unsalted roasted cashews
2 tablespoons fresh lime juice
1/3 cup olive oil
2 teaspoons sugar
Salt and freshly ground black pepper

Preparation
In a large bowl, combine the oranges, cashews, carrots, and cilantro and then set aside. In a small bowl, combine the sugar, orange, and lime juice and salt and pepper to taste. Whisk in the oil until blended. Pour the dressing over the carrot mixture, stirring to lightly coat. Toss gently to combine and serve.

French-Style Potato Salad

Preparation time: 15 minutes

Ingredients (5 servings)
1 1/2 pounds unpeeled small white potatoes
2 tablespoons minced fresh parsley
1 tablespoon minced fresh chives
1 teaspoon minced fresh tarragon
1/3 cup olive oil
2 tablespoons white wine or tarragon vinegar
1/2 teaspoon salt
1/8 teaspoon freshly ground black pepper
1/8 teaspoon sugar

Preparation
In a large pot of boiling salted water, cook the potatoes until tender but still firm, about 30 minutes. Drain and cut into 1/4-inch slices. Transfer to a large bowl and add the parsley, chives, and tarragon. Set aside. In a small bowl, combine the oil, vinegar, salt, pepper, and sugar. Pour the dressing onto the potato mixture and toss gently to combine. Taste, by adjusting the seasonings, if necessary. Chill for 1 to 2 hours before serving.

Desserts

Greek Butter Biscuits

Preparation time: 10 minutes
Cook time: 15 minutes

Ingredients (40 servings)
3/4 cup butter
3/4 cup granulated sugar
1 egg
2 egg yolks
3 1/2 cups flour
1 beaten egg
2 teaspoons baking powder
Cream butter and sugar

Preparation
Add the egg and egg yolks and beat until light and fluffy. Add flour, sifted with baking powder. Knead to make a soft dough, chill for an hour and form into small rings. Arrange on greased baking sheets, brush with beaten egg, and bake in a moderate oven for about 12 minutes.

Italian Cookies

Preparation time: 15 minutes
Cooking time: 20 minutes
Nutrition facts (per serving): 180 kcal (fats 11g, proteins 3g, fibers 0g)

Ingredients (22 cookies)
1 egg
½ cup of unsalted butter
½ cup of powdered sugar
½ teaspoon of almond extract
½ cup of almond flour
¼ teaspoon of salt
¼ cup of flour

Preparation
Preheat the oven to 350 F. Combine the butter and sugar until light and fluffy, whisk the egg, almond extract and salt in. After a minute, add the flour and almond flour and mix well. Scoop the mixture, roll it in your hands and then press down. Place on a baking tray and bake for 21-24 minutes. Dust with sugar and cool before serving.

Chocolate Balls

Preparation time: 15 minutes

Ingredients
1/2 pound walnut meats
1/2 pound sweet cooking chocolate
9 pieces zwieback
1 1/2 tablespoons granulated sugar
1/2 teaspoon cinnamon
2 tablespoons rose water
Confectioners' sugar

Preparation
Put walnut pieces, cooking chocolate and zwieback through the fine blade of a food chopper. Add rose water, sugar, and cinnamon. Form into 36 small balls. Roll in confectioners' sugar. Store the balls airtight.

Greek Rice Pudding

Preparation time: 15 minutes
Cook time: 20 minutes

Ingredients (7 servings)
1/2 cup short grain rice
1 cinnamon stick
6 cups milk
1 1/2 tablespoons cornstarch mixed with 2 tablespoons milk
1 teaspoon vanilla extract
1/2 cup sugar
Zest of 1 lemon
A grating of fresh nutmeg
2 cups water
Ground cinnamon (for garnish)

Preparation
Combine rice, cinnamon stick, and water in a saucepan and bring to a boil. Lower the heat and simmer covered for 15 minutes. Add the milk, cornstarch mixture, and sugar to the pan. Increase the heat to moderate and stir constantly 16 minutes, until the mixture thickens. Add lemon zest, vanilla extract, and nutmeg and stir to combine. Spoon into individual serving bowls or glasses and refrigerate for at least 2 hours. Dust with a little cinnamon before serving.

Amaretti Cookies

Preparation time: 15 minutes
Cooking time: 30 minutes

Ingredients (15 servings)
1 cup almond flour (or 3 cups finely ground almonds)
3 egg whites
½ teaspoon vanilla extract
1 teaspoon almond extract
1 cup fine sugar

Preparation
Preheat the oven to 300 F. In a food processor mix together the almond flour and sugar. Add the vanilla and almond extract and pulse for a few seconds. Add the egg whites, one at a time, and continue to process until the dough is smooth. Place the dough in teaspoonful amounts on baking paper on oven trays. Dust lightly with sugar. Bake for 25 - 30 minutes, depending on whether you prefer them slightly chewy or crispy. Store in a cool, dry container.

Sugar Cookies

Preparation time: 15 minutes
Cook time: 15 minutes
Nutrition facts (per serving): 121 kcal (3.9g fat, 4.8g protein, 2.8g fiber)

Ingredients (8 servings)

1/2-pound clarified butter cooled
1/2-pound powder sugar
1-pound (500g) flour
Halved almonds or pistachios

Preparation

At 325 degrees F, preheat the oven. Beat cold butter in a mixer for 2 minutes. Add sugar and continue beating until creamy. Stir in flour and beat until it makes a dough. Knead this dough and cover to refrigerate for 30 minutes. Make small, golf ball-sized balls from this mixture. Press each ball into a cookie and place the cookies in a greased baking sheet. Bake for almost 15 minutes in the preheated oven. Garnish with pistachios.

Syrian Harissa

Preparation time: 15 minutes
Cook time: 35 minutes
Nutrition facts (per serving): 369 kcal (12g fat, 10g protein, 4g fiber)

Ingredients (10 servings)
3 cups (1 pound/500g) coarse semolina
1 cup coconut flakes
1 cup yogurt
1 cup brown sugar
1 2/3 ounces (50g) butter
1 teaspoon baking powder
3 1/2 ounces (100g) almonds
3 cups brown sugar
1 ½ cups water
Juice of half a lemon
1 teaspoon flower water

Preparation
Mix yogurt, semolina, coconut, 1 cup brown sugar, baking powder, and butter in a bowl. Spread this mixture in a greased baking pan and bake for 30 minutes in the oven at 350 degrees F. Meanwhile, mix 3 cups of brown sugar with water, lemon juice, and flower water in a saucepan, then stir and cook until it thickens and the sugar is caramelized. Pour this syrup over the *harissa* and refrigerate it overnight. Slice and serve.

Syrian Milk Pudding

Preparation time: 15 minutes
Cook time: 10 minutes
Nutrition facts (per serving): 281 kcal (6g fat, 2.4g protein, 0.6g fiber)

Ingredients (8 servings)
4 cups (1 liter) almond milk
8 ounces (240 g) raw sugar
3 1/2 ounces (100 g) corn flour
1 tablespoon rose water
1 tablespoon orange blossom water
3 ounces (100 ml) cold water

Preparation
Mix cold water with corn flour in a bowl. Add almond milk, sugar, rose water, orange blossom water, and cornstarch to a saucepan over medium heat and mix well until thick and lump-free. Pour this pudding into a casserole dish and allow it to cool. Cover this pudding dish with a plastic wrap and then refrigerate until solid. Slice into cubes and garnish with pistachios.

Caramelized Dates

Preparation time: 15 minutes
Cook time: 10 minutes
Nutrition facts (per serving): 115 kcal (0.9g fat, 1g protein, 3g fiber)

Ingredients (6 servings)
8 ounces dates, pitted and chopped
1 teaspoon ghee
1 teaspoon sugar

Preparation
Melt ghee in a cooking pot and add dates then stir fry for 5-10 minutes until caramelized. Drizzle sugar on top and mix well. Serve.

Sunset Fruit Salad

Preparation time: 10 minutes

Ingredients (5 servings)
1 orange, peeled, sectioned, and cut into 1/2 -inch dice
1 banana, cut into ¼ -inch slices
1 peach or nectarine, halved, pitted, and cut into ½ -inch dice
2 tablespoons lemon juice
2 tablespoons agave nectar
1 Golden Delicious apple, unpeeled, cored, and cut into ½ -inch dice
1 cup pitted fresh cherries

Preparation
In a large bowl, combine the lemon juice and agave nectar, stirring to blend. Add the apple, banana, peach, orange, and cherries. Stir gently to combine, before serving.

Chocolate Mousse

Preparation time: 20 minutes

Ingredients
1 tablespoon light agave syrup 1/4 cup soymilk
½ cup unsweetened cocoa powder
1 (16 ounce) package silken tofu, drained
¾ cup stevia extract
1 teaspoon pure vanilla extract
2 tablespoons carob powder mint leaves

Preparation
Place tofu, Stevia extract, and vanilla in a food processor or blender. Process until well blended. Add remaining ingredients and process until the mixture is fully blended. Pour into small dessert cups. Chill for at least 150 minutes. Garnish with fresh mint leaves just before serving.

Turkish Baked Rice Pudding

Preparation Time: 20 minutes
Cooking Time: 20 minutes
Nutrition facts (per serving): 496 kcal

Ingredients (4 Servings)
2 tablespoons of cornstarch
1 egg yolk, beaten with 3 tablespoons of milk
½ cup of uncooked rice
4 ¾ cups of whole milk
1 cup of sugar
1 teaspoon of vanilla extract

Preparation
Preheat the oven to 350 F. Wash the rice and place it in a large saucepan with enough water to cover it by about ½ inch. Bring it to a boil and reduce the heat. Let the rice simmer gently for 4-6 minutes or until the rice is soft. Add 3 ¾ cups of milk, sugar and vanilla extract to the rice. Bring the mixture to a boil. Reduce the heat and let it boil very gently for about 11 minutes. Using a whisk, mix together the remaining 1 cup of the milk and the cornstarch, in a small bowl, until smooth. While stirring, gradually pour this mixture into the rice. Turn up the heat and continue stirring the pudding until scalding.

When the pudding thickens, continue to stir and cook for an additional 2 minutes. Remove from the heat and fill the small, ovenproof dessert cups, clay cups, or disposable aluminum pudding cups with the hot mixture. Using a spoon, drizzle a small amount of the egg yolk and milk mixture into the center of each dessert cup. With the back of the spoon, use a light, circular motion to swirl the egg yolk from the center to the edges so that it spreads evenly over the top of each cup. Bake the pudding cups until the tops are nicely browned, for about 20 minutes. Let the cups cool at room temperature and then refrigerate them for several hours before serving.

Kazandibi

Preparation Time: 10 minutes
Cooking Time: 40 minutes
Nutrition facts (per serving): 210 kcal

Ingredients (12 servings)
6 cups of milk
4 tablespoons of powdered sugar
1 teaspoon of cinnamon
3 tablespoons of rice flour
3 tablespoons of cornstarch
1 cup of granulated sugar
1 tablespoon of butter

Preparation
In a deep saucepan, combine the milk, granulated sugar, rice flour and cornstarch. Mix the mixture with a whisk until smooth and cook on the stove until thick. Add the butter, mix and let it melt in the dessert's temperature. Cover the entire surface of a greased baking sheet with a mixture of powdered sugar and cinnamon. Separate two scoops of the custard in equal amounts. Put the tray on the stove and pour one half of the mixture in it. When the burning process is over, pour the remaining custard into the tray. Fix it with a spatula. To raise the consistency, put in the fridge. Cut the dessert you have cooled into long thin slices and roll them up with a spatula.

Creamy Cocoa

Preparation time: 10 minutes

Ingredients
3 tablespoons canned coconut milk
½ teaspoon vanilla extract 3 tablespoons white sugar
4 ½ teaspoons cocoa powder
1 dash ground cinnamon
1 cup boiling water

Preparation
Stir together coconut milk, vanilla extract, sugar, cocoa powder, and cinnamon in a large mug. Add boiling water and stir until the sugar has dissolved.

Nirvana Chocolate Pudding

Preparation time: 20 minutes
Cook time: 25 minutes

Ingredients

3 tablespoons dry egg replacer
2 tablespoons cornstarch
1 cup soy creamer
1 cup soymilk
½ cup white sugar
3 ounces semisweet chocolate, chopped
2 teaspoons vanilla extract

Preparation

In a medium saucepan combine soymilk, cornstarch, and soy creamer and stir to dissolve cornstarch. Place on medium heat and stir in sugar. Cook, whisking frequently, until mixture comes to a low boil and then remove from heat. In a small bowl whisk egg replacer with 1/4 cup of hot milk mixture; return to pan with remaining milk mixture. Cook over medium heat 4 minutes until thick, but not boiling. Place the chocolate in a medium bowl and pour in the hot milk mixture. Let stand for 30 seconds, then stir until melted and smooth. Cool for 12-16 minutes, then stir in vanilla. Pour into ramekins or custard cups. Cover with plastic wrap and let cool at room temperature and then in the refrigerator for at least 2 hours.

Strawberry And Orange Skewers

Preparation: 20 minutes
Cook time: 10 minutes

Ingredients (4 servings)
8 large ripe strawberries, hulled
½ cup orange-flavored liqueur
2 large navel oranges, peeled and cut into 1-inch chunks

Preparation
Skewer the orange chunks and strawberries on 8 skewers, placing 2 or 3 orange chunks on each skewer, followed by 1 strawberry, and finishing with 2 or 3 pieces of orange. Place the skewered fruit in a shallow dish and pour liqueur over the fruit, turning to coat. Set aside for 70 minutes. Preheat the grill. Grill the fruit skewers, brushing with the marinade, about 3 minutes per side. Serve the skewers hot and drizzled with the remaining marinade.

Turkish Sweet Churros

Preparation Time: 5 minutes
Cooking Time: 30 minutes
Nutrition facts (per serving): 537 Cal

Ingredients (6 servings)
Dough
2 ½ cups of all-purpose flour
2 cups of water
2 oz of butter
1 teaspoon of sugar
1 pinch of salt
3 eggs
1 tablespoon of semolina
1 tablespoon of starch
2 cups of sunflower oil to fry

Syrup
1 tablespoon of lemon juice
4 cups of water
4 cups of sugar

Preparation
Heat the water in a saucepan and melt the unsalted butter in hot water. Add the flour and stir fast on a medium heat. Stir until it becomes soft and turns into a non-sticky dough. Remove from the flame, transfer the dough to another bowl and let it cool. While the dough is cooling down, prepare the sugar syrup. Pour 4 cups of water and sugar in a large pot and boil over a medium heat. When it starts to boil, add the lemon juice, turn the stove off and set aside. Take a cooled dough mixing bowl and begin mixing the eggs with a mixer. Add the semolina and starch and start adding your eggs gradually. Mix well until it becomes smooth. Fill your piping bag with the dough. Pipe the dough into frying oil.

When they have fully browned, take them out and directly transfer them into the sweet syrup. After 2 minutes, take them out of the syrup onto the plate.

Mint And Watermelon Ice Cream

Preparation time: 10 minutes

Ingredients (4 servings)
5 cups frozen watermelon
2 tablespoon maple syrup
1 cup coconut cream
A handful of fresh mint
Pinch of salt

Preparation
Combine all the ingredients in a blender or food processor. Blend and be sure to stop and scrape down the sides, as needed, until creamy and smooth. Eat immediately as soft serve or freeze for 4 hours until able to scoop.

Turkish Catal

Preparation Time: 20 minutes
Cooking Time: 20 minutes
Nutrition facts (per serving): 165 Cal

Ingredients (15 servings)
4 oz of soft margarine or butter
½ cup of low-fat yogurt
½ cup of whole yogurt
3 oz of olive oil
1 egg
1 tablespoon of sesame seeds/nigella seeds
1 pound of flour
1 tablespoon of sugar
¼ teaspoon of salt
2 tablespoons of vinegar
1 tablespoon of baking powder

Preparation
In a bowl, mix the yogurt, egg, margarine, vinegar and baking powder. Gradually add flour and mix until you get a non-sticky soft dough. Place the dough on a plain surface, divide into walnut-sized balls and roll each to a rope using hands. Now fold the cord to create a wide "S" shape, so that the width is about twice the height. Now pinch the sides of the S to develop an oval shape with three strands and lay them in a greased pan or a baking sheet. Mix an egg yolk with a teaspoon of oil and brush the pastries. Sprinkle the sesame seeds. Bake at 350 F for 18-22 minutes or until golden brown.

Persian Rice Cookies

Preparation time: 15 minutes
Cook time: 10 minutes
Nutrition facts (per serving): 120 kcal (Carbs 18 g, Fat 4 g, Protein 2 g)

Ingredients (90 servings)

Syrup
¼ teaspoon rosewater
¾ cup sugar

Cookies
1 cup rice flour
1/3 clarified butter
1 egg yolk
¾ teaspoon sugar
1 tablespoon poppy seeds
½ cardamom powder
2 ½ canola oil
¼ cup syrup

Preparation

Syrup
Pour the sugar and ¼ cup water into a saucepan over high heat. Mix the content 4-6 minutes or until the sugar melts. Take the pan away from the heat, add rosewater, and allow it cool down.

Cookies
Preheat the oven to 350F. Put the egg yolk and sugar into a bowl and mix until they blend consistently and then leave aside. Add clarified butter to another bowl together with oil, rice flour and cardamom. Pour the sugar and yolk mixture into the bowl and make sure they're evenly mixed and blended. Include the syrup and mix again. Let it cool. Mold the mixture into balls and put on a

parchment paper-lined baking sheet. The balls should be about 1/8 pounds and should be about ¾ inches thick. Flatten the balls by using a meat mallet or a fork. Scatter poppy seeds on them and bake for 11-13 minutes or until done. Cool down before serving.

Walnut Cake

Preparation time: 10 minutes
Cook time: 20 minutes
Nutrition facts (per serving): 160 kcal (Carbs 24 g, Fat 6g, Protein 3 g)

Ingredients (4 servings)
3 cup, pitted dates
1 ½ cup, sifted all-purpose flour
½ cup, powdered sugar
1 teaspoon ground cinnamon
½ teaspoon ground cardamom
1 cup, pistachios, ground unsalted
1 cup, walnuts, coarsely chopped
1 cup unsalted butter
Dough

Preparation
In a large skillet toast the walnuts for 6-7 minutes and then place them aside. Place some walnuts in the middle of the dates and lay them in the bottom of a serving dish. Put a large pan over medium heat and cook the flour with butter for 18-20 minutes or until they become golden brown over high heat. Pour the hot mix all over the dates and spread it. In a small mixing bowl, mix in it the cinnamon, sugar and cardamom. Sprinkle the mix all over the butter and flour layer, followed by the pistachios. Place the cake aside to lose heat and add your preferred topping to taste.

If you liked these easy recipes, discover to how cook DELICIOUS recipes from Balkan countries!

Within these pages, you'll learn 35 authentic recipes from a Balkan cook. These aren't ordinary recipes you'd find on the Internet, but recipes that were closely guarded by our Balkan mothers and passed down from generation to generation.

Main Dishes, Appetizers, and Desserts included!

If you want to learn how to make Croatian green peas stew, and 32 other authentic Balkan recipes, then start with our book!

Order at www.balkanfood.org/cook-books now for only $2,99

If you're a Mediterranean dieter who wants to know the secrets of the Mediterranean diet, dieting, and cooking, then you're about to discover how to master cooking meals on a Mediterranean diet right now!

In fact, if you want to know how to make Mediterranean food, then this new e-book - "The 30-minute Mediterranean diet" - gives you the answers to many important questions and challenges every Mediterranean dieter faces, including:
- How can I succeed with a Mediterranean diet?
- What kind of recipes can I make?
- What are the key principles to this type of diet?
- What are the suggested weekly menus for this diet?
- Are there any cheat items I can make?

... and more!

If you're serious about cooking meals on a Mediterranean diet and you really want to know how to make Mediterranean food, then you need to grab a copy of "The 30-minute Mediterranean diet" right now.

Prepare **111 recipes with several ingredients in less than 30 minutes**!

Order at www.balkanfood.org/cook-books for only $2,99!

What could be better than a home-cooked meal? Maybe only a Greek homemade meal.

Do not get discouraged if you have no Greek roots or friends. Now you can make a Greek food feast in your kitchen.

This ultimate Greek cookbook offers you 111 best dishes of this cuisine! From more famous gyros to more exotic *Kota Kapama* this cookbook keeps it easy and affordable.

All the ingredients necessary are wholesome and widely accessible.
The author's picks are as flavorful as they are healthy. The dishes described in this cookbook are "what Greek mothers have made for decades."

Full of well-balanced and nutritious meals, this handy cookbook includes many vegan options. Discover a plethora of benefits of Mediterranean cuisine, and you may fall in love with cooking at home.

Inspired by a real food lover, this collection of delicious recipes will taste buds utterly satisfied.

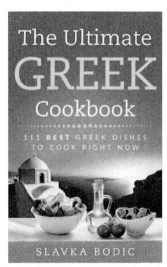

Order at www.balkanfood.org/cook-books for only $2,99!

Maybe to try exotic Syrian cuisine?

From succulent *sarma*, soups, warm and cold salads to delectable desserts, the plethora of flavors will satisfy the most jaded foodie. Have a taste of a new culture with this **traditional Serbian cookbook**.

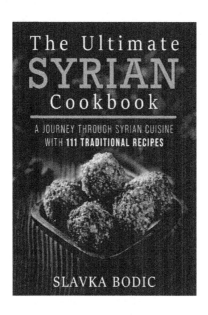

Order at www.balkanfood.org/cook-books for only $2,99!

ONE LAST THING

If you enjoyed this book or found it useful, I'd be very grateful if you could find the time to post a short review on Amazon. Your support really does make a difference and I read all the reviews personally, so I can get your feedback and make this book even better.

Thanks again for your support!

Please send me your feedback at:

www.balkanfood.org

Printed in Great Britain
by Amazon